Bible Study Guide: Habakkuk

Ancient Words Bible Study Series

Andrew J. Lamont-Turner

Published by Andrew J. Lamont-Turner, 2024.

BIBLE STUDY GUIDE: HABAKKUK

First edition. April 19, 2024.

ISBN: 979-8224571666

Written by Andrew J. Lamont-Turner.

Table of Contents

To God be all the Glory.

I pray for God's blessing upon you as you study the material. May He open your mind to receive this information and live by it.

Andrew

Study Guide: Habakkuk
Verse-By-Verse Study of the Bible Book of Habakkuk
Copyright Andrew J Lamont-Turner 2023
First Edition: 2023

Scripture quotations, unless otherwise stated, are taken from the New Covenant Theological Seminary Grammatically Corrected Contemporary English Bible®, Copyright © 2023 by New Covenant Theological Seminary. Used under license.

Scripture references marked WEB have been taken from the World English Bible. Public Domain.

The author uses Google Translate to translate this study into various languages, with English as the original language.

Cover Page Design by AJ Lamont-Turner
Photography by
Jess Du Toit Photography
jessejdt@gmail.com

Foreword

As we live increasingly complex and uncertain lives, the book Habakkuk offers a powerful message of hope and perseverance. Through the prophet Habakkuk's questioning and dialogue with God, we are reminded of the importance of faith and trust in God, even in the face of injustice and violence.

The book of Habakkuk is a reminder that our faith is tested in the face of difficult circumstances, and how we react to those circumstances is key. Many of us can relate to Habakkuk's question, "Yahweh, for how much longer am I going to cry, and you will not hear?" (Habakkuk 1:2). But Habakkuk's ultimate trust in God's sovereignty and justice is a powerful example.

As you read this book, you will see how Habakkuk's message of hope and perseverance is timeless and relevant. The author has done an excellent job of bringing Habakkuk's message to life. The insights will help you better understand this ancient prophet's message and how it can be applied to our modern world.

This book is not just for those already well-versed in the Bible but for anyone seeking to deepen their understanding of faith and trust in God. It is a powerful reminder that we can find hope and joy in God even in the darkest times. I highly recommend this book to anyone looking to strengthen their faith and find guidance in difficult times.

Andrew

Introduction to this Study

This study comprises questions based on the various verses of Scripture taken from the Book of Habakkuk.

Part 1 of this study explores the background information of the book, for example, who wrote it, when, to whom, why and other aspects of the book.

Part 2 is the verse-by-verse study that requires the reader to complete the questions and tasks at the end of each chapter. If this is done in a cell group environment, these answers should be discussed within the group.

Part 3 comprises questions based on the whole book of Habakkuk to test your knowledge. After all the chapters have been studied, there are true, false, and multi-choice questions to test your knowledge of this book.

Suppose you are using the ebook version of this study. In that case, it is advisable to have a notebook handy to record the answers to the questions. Additional space may also be required to work through the test your knowledge questions.

Answering the questions is not a race. Careful thought should go into writing down the answers, specifically the life application of these questions and their answers.

Engaging in a Bible Study suggests that the reader recognises their need to understand Scripture and the depth of wisdom that follows knowing and understanding God and His ways. This is a spiritual journey, and it takes time as you investigate the verses, their meaning as the writer intended them to be, and their life application. Ensure prayer precedes each step of the way, allowing the Holy Spirit to guide you and opening your heart and mind to the knowledge of God.

This study matters as it might apply to your life's reality. In other words, this study considers the Book's Theology and other principles derived from the book within a framework that makes it easier to apply principles to our daily lives. This study is not a commentary, and although specific information about each book is provided, this study does not engage in textual criticism.

PART 1: Book Information

Book Title & Writer

The author's surname is also the title of the book they wrote. There is some debate over what the name Habakkuk really means. It may originate from the Hebrew word habaq, translated as "to fold the hands" or "to embrace." The second scenario might indicate "one who embraces" or "one who is embraced." Luther believed it to be a symbol that Habakkuk consoled and supported his people by enveloping them in his arms. Jerome understood it to imply that the speaker was taking responsibility for the issue of divine justice worldwide, which is the book's central theme.

Regarding Habakkuk, we can only say that he was a prophet who existed during the pre-exilic era of Israel's history, which occurred in the seventh century B.C. Only Haggai and Zechariah, the only other prophets who wrote, are referred to by the mere name "the prophet" (1:1). This identification is not accompanied by any additional distinguishing feature. Habakkuk's book is the only one to be given this designation among the prophets who lived before the exile. The book's contents, which point to Habakkuk's status as a poet and prophet, include wisdom literature and a hymn that praises the Lord. It has been said that "the freethinker among the prophets" describes him best.

The authors of the New Testament provided us with no information concerning Habakkuk. Some legends have been passed down about who he was, but they have little truth. Nonetheless, they are fascinating to learn about. Other scholars concluded that he was a musician and probably a Levite because the last stanza of the book has a musical notation comparable to some psalms.

The apocryphal book Bel and the Dragon is included in the Septuagint. Its title refers to Habakkuk as "the son of Jeshua of the tribe of Levi." This addition was made to the Book of Daniel and is included in the Septuagint.

It relates to an entirely fictitious myth about Habakkuk. It is said that an angel gave Habakkuk the order to bring food to Daniel as he was imprisoned in the lions' den for the second time. After hearing the prophet's complaint that he could not locate the cave, the angel took hold of a strand of the man's hair and led him directly to the hiding place (Bel vv. 33-39).

According to the teachings of the rabbis, Habakkuk was the son of a Shunammite lady whose life Elisha had brought back to her (2 Kings 4). This hypothesis is based on the fact that Elisha's servant promised the lady in 2 Kings 4:16 that she would "embrace" a son. Habakkuk is close to the Hebrew term translated as "embrace." This provides the foundation for this argument.

Location

As Habakkuk prophesied when the Chaldeans were on the ascent, we might deduce that the prophet resided in Judah. The invasion of Israel by the Assyrians in 722 B.C. ended the existence of the Northern Kingdom of Israel. As a result, Habakkuk was a prophet of the Southern Kingdom who lived during a period when degeneration, vulnerability, and terror were on the rise.

Writer

Habakkuk was a prophet who lived during the pre-exilic era of Israel's history, which occurred in the seventh century B.C. Only Haggai and Zechariah, the only other prophets who wrote, are referred to by the mere name "the prophet" (1:1). This identification is not accompanied by any additional distinguishing feature. Habakkuk's book is the only one to be given this designation among the prophets who lived before the exile. The book's contents, which point to Habakkuk's status as a poet and a prophet, include pieces of wisdom literature and a hymn that praises the Lord. It has been said of him that "the freethinker among the prophets" describes him best.

The authors of the New Testament provided us with no information concerning Habakkuk. Some traditions have been passed down about who he was that have very little truth in reality but are nonetheless fascinating to learn about. Several scholars concluded that he was a musician and probably a Levite because the last stanza of the book has a musical notation comparable to that of other psalms.

The apocryphal book Bel and the Dragon is included in the Septuagint. Its title refers to Habakkuk as "the son of Jeshua of the tribe of Levi." This addition was made to the Book of Daniel and is included in the Septuagint.

It relates to a myth about Habakkuk that is entirely fictitious, saying things like It is said that an angel gave Habakkuk the order to bring food to Daniel as he was imprisoned in the lions' den for the second time. After hearing the prophet's complaint that he could not locate the cave, the angel took hold of a strand of the man's hair and led him directly to the hiding place (Bel vv. 33-39).

According to the teachings of the rabbis, Habakkuk was the son of a Shunammite lady whose life Elisha had brought back to her (2 Kings 4). This hypothesis is based on the fact that Elisha's servant promised the lady in 2 Kings 4:16 that she would "embrace" a son. The name Habakkuk is close to the Hebrew term that is translated as "embrace." This provides the foundation for this argument.

Date of Writing

The book has references that assist us in roughly dating it. Still, these references make it hard to be accurate or dogmatic. Habakkuk was instructed by the LORD (Yahweh) that He was resurrecting the Chaldeans (also known as Neo-Babylonians), a ferocious and impulsive people who were already moving over the whole world and that they would extend their empire much farther (1:6). Nabopolassar was the first monarch to rule over the Neo-Babylonian civilisation (627-605 B.C.). This reference alludes to a period before 605 B.C., when Babylon destroyed the combined armies of Egypt and Assyria in the battle of Carchemish, establishing itself as the dominant power in the ancient Near East. It may be possible to point to a period before the Babylonians and the Medes and Scythians destroyed Nineveh in 612 B.C.

However, numerous allusions in the Bible that describe the circumstances in ancient Judah and the Near East lend credence to the notion that the event took place between 608 and 605 B.C. (cf. 1:7-11). The fall of the Judean monarchy, which started with the death of King Josiah in the year 609 B.C. and is discussed in Habakkuk, provides the context for the book. This places the publication of the book at around the year 605 B.C. Since King Jehoiakim governed Judah from 609 to 598 B.C., Habakkuk likely prophesied during his reign (cf. 2 Kings 23:36–24:7; 2 Chronicles 36:5-8). This view is held by the vast majority of evangelical experts.

On the one hand, Habakkuk predicted the Babylonians' ascent to power and prominence as a shock (1:5-6). On the other hand, the prophecy assumes that the Babylonians had already established a reputation for being an imperialistic empire (see 1:6-11, 15-17; 2:5-17). Understanding the book as a compilation of messages from various periods during the prophet's career is the most effective method for finding a solution to the dilemma.

Another author felt that some oracles date back to before 605 B.C. In comparison, others arrived after 597 B.C., and the final shape of the book reflected Habakkuk's post-597 B.C. viewpoint. This belief was supported by the fact that some oracles are dated.

While it seems complicated to pinpoint the exact dates of Habakkuk's ministry, it is believed that he served as a prophet for several years before Jerusalem was destroyed in 586 B.C. by Nebuchadnezzar.

Purpose for Writing & Audience

Habakkuk preached to Judeans, who seemed to be living during the era of King Jehoiakim. These Judeans were called the "people to whom he ministered." During his reign, the Israelites sought assistance in the wrong areas, namely Egypt and Assyria. This was a mistake since Babylonian dominance was expanding during this time. They should have been looking mainly to the LORD. Their inability to do so was one of the difficulties that Jeremiah, who lived at the same time as Habakkuk, carried.

Both Jeremiah and Habakkuk lived during the same period. Jeremiah preached that evil among God's chosen people would ultimately fail. In contrast, Habakkuk taught that wickedness among the Chaldeans would likewise fail. The roots of tyranny are always inside the system, waiting to sprout.

On the other hand, Habakkuk's worries were more intellectual than Jeremiah's. What troubled him was that the all-powerful LORD was not reacting to the wickedness of Habakkuk's time and the internal injustices it perpetrated. He prayed to Yahweh, expressing his concerns to him (1:2-4). The LORD responded by saying that He was hard at work. He was establishing a country that would serve as a chastisement for disobeying His people against the terms of the covenant (1:5-11). This presented Habakkuk with a new challenge, which he prayed over before bringing to the LORD: How could the LORD punish God's chosen people by using a country that was even more evil than Judah (1:12–2:1)? The LORD made it clear that He will one day exact retribution against the Babylonians for their own acts of depravity (2:2-20). The last chapter is a song of praise that extols Yahweh for His understanding of human nature. Therefore, the book's goal was to demonstrate that God is righteous and give the people of God reason to have hope and encouragement.

His primary theme is that which preoccupied Asaph in the 73rd Psalm, namely the sorrows of the upright amid the affluence of the wicked. The response is always the same; the consequence of everything will be one massive turnaround, with the wicked bringing misfortune upon themselves and God rewarding the patience of the virtuous by instilling obedience to His holy will.

Habakkuk was the only one of the twelve minor prophets to engage the issue of evil in a disordered society with the same level of sincerity as the others. What are godly people supposed to do when their society's political and social institutions are falling apart. At the same time, is their nation's moral and spiritual fibre being torn apart? This is the distressing subject that the prophet Habakkuk addresses in his writings.

Until the day that God avenges the Babylonians and restores Jerusalem, the righteous life by faith (Hab. 2:1-4), having to wait with confidence for the fulfilment of I AM's unfaltering promise that the wrongdoers will be destroyed (2:5-19) and that his genuine claim to the entire world will be universally recognised (Hab. 2:1-4). (3:1-16).

Place of Writing

Since Habakkuk prophesied when the Chaldeans were on the ascent, we might deduce that the prophet resided in Judah. The invasion of Israel by the Assyrians in 722 B.C. ended the existence of the Northern Kingdom of Israel. As a result, Habakkuk was a prophet of the Southern Kingdom who lived when degeneration, vulnerability, and terror were on the rise.

Special Features

This work makes use of several different literary styles. A conversation between Habakkuk and his God is found in the book's opening section (1:2–2:5). It moves back and forth between Habakkuk expressing his sadness and God making a heavenly proclamation. The second section is a song of taunting or mockery that the prophet instructed the countries oppressed by Babylon to sing. These nations had previously been victims of Babylon's rule. It is made up of a total of five "woes" (2:6-20). The third section is a psalm with suggestions for musical accompaniment (ch. 3). As Jonah's story was presented in prose, this book is the prophet's personal experience written in poetry. Jonah's story was told in prose.

Habakkuk is a remarkable book. In contrast to previous prophets who communicated God's word to humanity, this prophet conversed with God regarding those individuals. Most prophets in the Old Testament spoke of the impending wrath of God. Habakkuk asked for divine judgment. In contrast to the conventional accusation, this short book chronicles a fascinating conversation between a confused prophet and his Maker. The conversation between Habakkuk and God is the foundation for the book's whole structure and intellectual process.

Again, unlike the other prophets, Habakkuk is not as concerned with delivering a message as he is with finding a solution to a problem. This issue troubled his sensitive soul and was related to Jehovah's administration of the nations.

The prophet posed some of the most insightful questions in written form. The solutions to these questions are fundamental to developing an accurate understanding of God and his place in history unfolding. If God's first response actually sounds like the death knell for any tightly nationalistic covenant theology of Judah, then his second response outlined in a positive sense the fact that all of history was expediting to a conclusion that was [just as] sure as it was satisfying. If God's first response sounded like the beginning of the end for any strictly ethnocentric covenant theology of Judah, then his second reply sounded like the death knell for any strictly The virtuous are to live their lives by faith in the interval, while history is still waiting for its conclusion (although Habakkuk was not informed when the end will come, obviously for him prefigured by Babylon's fall). The prescribed faith, or "faithfulness," as many have argued that the Hebrew word "emunah" should be translated, is still considered a primary reaction to the questions left unanswered today. This, a theology for life then and now, continues to stand as Habakkuk's most fundamental contribution.

There are many parallels between the books of Nahum, Habakkuk, and Zephaniah. Each reveals a unique aspect of how God has dealt with humanity throughout history. They illustrate how the administration of God is incorporated into the rule of society. They also reveal how God has dealt with the person.

If Zephaniah emphasised humility and spiritual poverty as necessary for coming into the advantages of the company of the believing, Habakkuk required faith as the most essential condition for entering into the benefits of the believing. But they are all interconnected pieces of the same puzzle. Habakkuk was troubled by the growing lawlessness, injustice, immorality, and rebellion in the land, whilst Zephaniah emphasised the idolatry and religious syncretism of the people of Judah.

The Edomites, the Assyrians, and the Chaldeans or Babylonians were the most notable adversaries that plagued the people of the covenant in ancient times. It was entrusted to three Hebrew prophets in particular so that they might prophesy the destruction of these three powers. The destiny of Edom was determined by Obadiah's prophecy. The words of Nahum's prophesy rang out as the death bell for Assyria. The prophecy of Habakkuk was the shovel that finally put Babylon to rest.

Habakkuk Practically Applied

The book of Habakkuk is unique among the prophetic literature in that it is written as a story. This is one way in which it is comparable to the book of Jonah, which is similarly the account of the experiences of a prophet. The book of Jonah recounts the story of a prophet who could not have compassion for God. The book of Habakkuk tells the experience of a prophet who could not comprehend God. Jonah and Habakkuk are tasked with solving problems presented by their respective cities: Jonah by Nineveh and Habakkuk by Babylon. Like Jonah, Habakkuk documents a significant turning point in the prophet's life. The vast majority of the other prophetic texts record the words and deeds of a prophet throughout a considerable amount of time. Because it does include prophecies, Habakkuk is comparable to the other books of the prophetic canon in this regard.

Verse 2:4 is regarded as the most crucial passage in the book. It reads: "Look! His spirit has become inflated with pride. Even if he does not have integrity, the virtue will be sustained by his faith."

This passage alludes to Habakkuk's challenge and includes the proclamation that Habakkuk made after he had been wrestling with his faith.

The book of Habakkuk is a collection of questions and answers posed by a prophet. Consider verse (1:2), which contains the first inquiry posed by the prophet. Then, at 3:19, he provides his concluding confirmation, having already received responses. The two verses give a stunning contrast to one another. The lament of despair stands in comparison to the yell of confidence that accompanies it.

The book of Habakkuk is structured as follows. At the outset, we have the perspective of a believer who doubts God. The prophet was challenged to understand why God was not fulfilling what He had promised to do, more particularly, why God was not saving His people from the bloodshed threatened by the Babylonians. Every believer will, at some point or another, struggle with the same issue. The promises of God are tested by the circumstances, and we wonder why God does not act to change the circumstances. Habakkuk was perplexed by the idea that God would chastise the corrupt Judahites via the means of an even more evil country, Babylon.

The most important verse, which is 2:4, may be compared to the narrow section of an hourglass: Everything that came before it served as preparation for it, and everything that came after it was a direct consequence of what it had started. It is comparable to a passageway through which all of the events in the book take place. This passage presents two perspectives on life that are diametrically opposed to one another: To begin, there is a person who is bloated, arrogant, and egotistical. Second, we have a believer who is brimming with confidence. The first person is filled with oneself or herself, whereas the second is filled with God. The distinction is in one's mentality: having high trust in oneself or faith in God. In each scenario, there is something that is concealed and made visible.

When someone is prideful, something about his soul or inner man is not balanced or aligned inside him. It is not right side up or even, but somewhat crooked or twisted. This is an abnormal state for him to be in. His actual situation, concealed from view, is one of crookedness of spirit, while his outward, apparent condition is one of conceit or pride. He is completely wrapped up in himself, and because he is wholly wrapped up in himself, one might say that he is completely wound up in a ball and is all twisted up inside. Notably, the poem does not mention what happens to prideful people. Our only information about him is that he was twisted and bloated.

When someone is virtuous, they have a pure soul inside herself. His actual, underlying state is that of being straight. Trust in God is the outward evidence of his state. As a side note, there is only one kind of straightness, but there are many types of crookedness and perversity. If I asked a group of individuals to see a straight stick, everyone would picture an unbent stick with no curves or bends. However, if I asked them to see a crooked stick somehow, each person's mental image would take on its own kind of crookedness. A crooked stick might be twisted in a hundred ways, but there is only one way a stick could be straight. While goodness may be summed up in a few short words, evil is a highly complex concept. Goodness may take only one form, yet evil can manifest itself in various ways.

The last phrase of verse 4 of Habakkuk is the most critical affirmation in the book. It says, "The righteous one will live by his faith." This affirmation centres on three main ideas: being virtuous, living a life of faith, and having confidence in God. Notably, the emphasis is placed on a different word in each of the three instances in the New Testament where this passage is mentioned. These instances are found in the following:

The word "righteous." is given a lot of attention in verse 17 of Romans. Paul's primary focus in Romans was on the righteousness of God and how individuals might achieve it. In verse found in Hebrews 10:38, the word "live." is highlighted. The author of the letter to the Hebrews emphasised the significance of following religion as a way of life rather than returning to Judaism and adhering to the Mosaic Law as a way of life. And in Galatians 3:11, the word "faith." is given primary prominence. In Galatians' book, Paul compares being saved by works and faith. As a result, the earlier remark has a lot of weight and significance. In fact, many people who study the Bible think that this verse sums up the most important idea that can be found in the whole book. It has been compared to the famous verse "John 3:16" in the New Testament.

Now, let us connect this to Habakkuk's witnessing, which caused him to struggle with his faith. He saw the blooming of pride. He was surrounded by unethical behaviour in a hundred varied guises and saw it everywhere. In addition, he saw the virtuous, who had faith in God, being harassed, threatened, and persecuted. In particular, he saw that the arrogant Babylonians, who denied the existence of Yahweh, were accumulating an increasing amount of authority. They seemed to be the only ones who were still alive. He watched as the people of God, who put their faith in Yahweh, gradually lost more and more of their influence.

It looked like they were going to die, and it was possible that they would become extinct. And what troubled Habakkuk the most was that God seemed to be doing nothing.

When the prophet was at the lowest point in his faith, God talked to him and revealed the profound meaning of verse 4. Despite appearances, faith is the principle that leads to life. At the same time, pride is the principle that leads to destruction, and faith is the principle that leads to life. The godless people and their schemes seem to be so powerful and unstoppable. Their endeavours, often disobeying God, give the impression that they are destined to succeed. Despite this, the person God considers virtuous because they relied on God will continue to exist.

What exactly is God up to? Despite what it may seem, he is causing everything to fall into place in a way consistent with the concept described in verse 4. The Sovereign of the Universe frequently takes millennia to work out His plans. While we desire Him to accomplish them in years, if not months, the Sovereign of the Universe has everything in His hand. He will make good on his commitments. He will reward faith. He will bring down those who are corrupt and arrogant.

The book's last section, after verse 2, allows us to see the results of trusting God's revelation in verse 2. Habakkuk went through a few depraved expressions of evil and then announced their complete and utter destruction. He also saw the history of the Israelites as a testimony to the truth of the central affirmation of the book. He shook with fear as he predicted what God had already done in the past and what He would do to the Chaldeans. He saw the history of the Israelites as a testimony to the truth of the central affirmation of the book. The prophet, who first believed that God was doing nothing, concluded by asking that Yahweh would remember kindness when He poured forth His wrath. This contrasts with the prophet's initial belief that God was doing nothing. As soon as he learned that he could continue to trust God despite how things seemed, he burst out into a hymn of praise. He had been under the impression that God had forgotten about the faithful.

The book of Habakkuk comes to a close not with a lament but with a song. It concludes with an assertion rather than an inquiry as its last step. It does not end with disappointment but rather with faith: 3:17-18. The book of Habakkuk imparts to those who read it several timeless and valuable truths, including the following:

One of the most essential takeaways from this book is that even devout believers might struggle to maintain their faith and confidence in God. If we look at what is happening today, we can come to the same conclusions that Habakkuk did at the beginning of this book and ask the same questions. While we await for God to award the righteous with life for their faith, we may have peace in our hearts and music on our lips if we continue to listen to the Word of God. If we continue listening to the Word of God, we can sing. This fundamental truth holds true on two levels: the level of justification and the level of sanctification.

Simply putting your faith and reliance on God is the only method to be considered righteous in his eyes (to be justified). In addition, the only way to maintain a righteous position before God (also known as progressive sanctification) is to continue to believe in Him despite what others see around you. This is possible for us because God has a perfect track record of keeping the promises that He has made, and the Bible is the record of that faithfulness. Therefore, rather than basing our lives on the lessons we have learned from experience, we need to look to the Bible for guidance. The covenants and promises of God are a more reliable indicator of truth than the present conditions.

We also need to be cautious not to slip into the group of the proud, who are consumed with thoughts of themselves and their accomplishments. We, too, are ready to go to the arrogant of this world for answers, even if they do not bend before God. Instead, we should demonstrate our righteousness by persevering in our faith in God despite what it may seem like to others. These days, people are more likely to put their confidence in scientific explanations than in the specific words found in the Bible. Where shall we place our confidence? We have no intention of joining the ranks of those perverted and mocking individuals whose goal is not life but death instead. It is important to note that several of the supposedly "assured facts" in the scientific community are now being questioned by members of the scientific community itself.

Notice how Habakkuk responded to the questions he was asked. It would have been possible for him to arrange a series of speaking engagements over Judah to demonstrate how incoherent God's rule over human affairs was. Thankfully, he prayed to God instead of asking others about his concerns and inquiries. God's response was to provide him with the answers. Habakkuk was the one who received the revelation from God. The prophet took the time to hear what God had to say. When we pray to God, we can bring him anything. Prayer is the most effective way to get our concerns and inquiries to God. The Bible, God's written word, is the finest place to look for God's answers. Some believe that God does not communicate as he did in times past. It is more accurate to argue that people do not listen to God as they did in the past. Becoming individuals devoted to praying and studying the Bible is essential to living by faith.

In addition, the mental state constantly reflects itself in the behaviour one displays externally. This is the case regardless of whether or not the internal attitude is of faith or pride. What does our behaviour toward the outside world reveal about how we feel on the inside? Whom should we put our trust in, God or man? Where should we look first if we are looking for answers? Do you believe in "authorities" other than the Bible?

In verse 3, God stated, "Though it [the vision, God's explanation] delays, wait for it; For it will certainly come." This refers to the vision as well as God's explanation. Being people of faith requires us to accept that we will have to wait for answers, whether in words or experiences that can only be gained in the future. Someone wise once stated that Christians are not people who live by explanations but instead by God's promises. We have no choice but to be happy with God's assurance that we will one day comprehend what is now incomprehensible.

To a significant extent, it is unknown how God will bring about the fulfilment of his purpose. Prophecy merely gives us a general overview of His acts. Still, here and there, it will disclose some astonishingly exact specifics. However, for the most part, we must be ready to hold on to our patience. Those who do not give up waiting on God will eventually get the life he promised them. The most challenging task is waiting, but like Habakkuk, we can sing even as we wait if we continue to speak to God and listen to what God has to say.

Outline

Conclusion

The prophet Habakkuk opens the book of Habakkuk by appealing to God for an explanation as to why the suffering of God's chosen people is permitted to continue throughout their captivity (Habakkuk 1:1–4). The Lord responds to Habakkuk with a statement that might be interpreted as "even if I told you, you still would not believe it" (Habakkuk 1:5–11). After that, Habakkuk continued by stating, "Fine, you are Yahweh; but, still, tell me more about why this is occurring" (Habakkuk 1:17—2:1). God then responds to him once again and provides him with further knowledge before commanding the world to remain quiet before him (Habakkuk 2:2–20). Then Habakkuk composes a prayer to convey his unwavering trust in God, even amid all these difficulties (Habakkuk 3:1–19).

The notion of being justified only based on one's faith is restated by the apostle Paul using a verse from Habakkuk (2:4) on two separate occasions (Romans 1:17 and Galatians 3:11). The faith that is a gift from God and may be obtained through Christ is both a saving faith (Ephesians 2:8–9) and a faith that continues to be a source of strength throughout one's whole life. Faith is how we get everlasting life, and faith is also how we live the Christian life. The one whose soul is not right inside him (Habakkuk 2:4, NASB) and whose inclinations are not straight (NIV) stands in contrast to the "proud." The one who is made righteous by faith in Christ opposes both. That individual's guilt was substituted for Christ's holiness (2 Corinthians 5:21). Since Christ has made it possible for him to live by faith, he now has a pure spirit inside him, and his aspirations are honourable. The person who has been redeemed is not haughty but is humble (see Matthew 5:5). He is a disciple of the Lord Jesus, who is described as "meek and lowly in heart" (Matthew 11:29).

The lesson that the reader of Habakkuk should take away from this passage is that it is OK to question what God is doing, provided that they do so with reverence and respect. Sometimes, what is going on is unclear, particularly if we are forced to endure hardship for an extended period or if our adversaries are thriving while we are only scraping by on the edge of survival. The book of Habakkuk provides evidence that God is both sovereign and almighty and has complete dominion over the universe. All that is required of us is to stay quiet and trust that He is at work. He is exactly who He claims to be and keeps the promises he makes. He will bring vengeance onto the wicked. Even when we cannot perceive proof of God's reign, we may be certain that he is still seated on the throne of the cosmos. We must keep this in mind at all times: "Yahweh, the Lord, is my source of strength. He transforms my feet into the feet of deer and gives me the ability to go to lofty heights" (Habakkuk 3:19). To "tread on the heights" is a metaphor for our capacity, by the power of God, to ascend above the challenges and obstructions of this world and achieve triumph over our foes. Sometimes, the path ahead of us is fraught with anguish and distress, but if we have faith in the Lord, we shall arrive safely at the destination that he has in mind.

PART 2: Verse-By-Verse Study

Habakkuk Chapter 1:1-17

1:1 The revelation that was made known to the prophet Habakkuk.

According to the author, this book was a revelation made known to Habakkuk, the prophet. This word, which the LORD put on Habakkuk as a burden (Hebrew: masse, which literally means "something lifted up"), was a prophecy forecasting judgement on Judah and Babylon. The prophecy of Habakkuk is marked by a weighty quality from the beginning to the end.

Nothing else we are absolutely definite about Habakkuk other than that he was a genuine prophet of the LORD who could also create poetry (ch. 3).

Habakkuk is referred to as the prophet, much as Haggai and Zechariah are at the beginning of the writings that bear their names (Hag. 1:1; Zech. 1:1). This suggests that Habakkuk was a trained prophet who worked for the temple administration. These temple prophets guided the congregation in their worship of God (cf. 1 Chron. 25:1). When a worshipper came to the temple seeking divine direction, it was the temple prophet's responsibility to respond to their questions. After hearing the question, the prophet would consult with God to determine the solution. This did not necessarily mean getting new instructions from God at every turn. It is likely that, in most instances, it included recounting what God had already revealed. It is possible that Habakkuk attached the term "the prophet" to his name rather than giving it as a separate title since he publicly expostulates with God like the Psalmists. Still, he does not speak in the name of God to the people.

Habakkuk's Complaint

1:2 Yahweh, for how much longer am I going to cry, and you will not hear? I call in distress to you, "Violence!" but you will not come to my rescue, will you not?

During his time of prayer, the prophet questioned Yahweh, asking "how long" it would be until the LORD would reply to his repeated pleas for assistance (cf. 2:6; Exodus 16:28; Numbers 14:11). 4 However, Habakkuk lamented that God had not offered proof of listening by replying to his request, even though God is omniscient and hence able to hear all prayers. He had implored the LORD, reminding him of the bloodshed he had seen in Judah, but the LORD had not come to Judah's rescue (cf. Genesis 6:11, 13; Job 19:7).

Like the suffering patriarch, he struggled with the difficult dilemma of allowing evil. Like Job, he found peace through an overpowering revelation of the glory of the Lord. Habakkuk was a Job among the prophets.

In the Old Testament, whenever justice (Hebrew: mishpat) and violence (Hebrew: hamas) are shown as being in opposition to one another, as they are here, the wicked are often depicted as being the Israelites unless they are specified explicitly as being outsiders (e.g., Exodus 23:1-9; Isaiah 5:7-15). It seemed as if God had not listened, and it is clear that He had not assisted the prophet.

Habakkuk turned to God with his sincere uncertainty rather than to any other "brain trust" of ordinary humans. If only we would do that instead of moaning our uncertainties into the ears of human beings, imagine how much unease we might avoid!

1:3 Why are you looking at perversity and showing me acts of iniquity? Because I face devastation and bloodshed here and now. There is conflict, and the level of discontent is rising.

Habakkuk was perplexed as to why Yahweh was permitting the calamity and famine he was forced to see daily to persist in the land of Judah. Not only were instances of destruction, violence, struggle, and dispute not uncommon, but they were also on the rise. But Yahweh did not intervene in the matter in any way.

The Hebrew word for "Violence" is hamas, and it appears six times in the book Habakkuk. This is an exceptionally high frequency for a book that is so brief. The Hebrew term for "conflict" refers to more than simply physical violence. It refers to a blatant transgression of the moral rule committed by someone that causes harm to their fellow man (e.g., Genesis 6:11). It refers to any behaviour that violates ethical standards. Physical assault is only one example of this. Habakkuk emphasised the severity of the tyranny that was taking place in Judah by using a variety of synonyms for the word "injustice."

This is not an incident in which the earthen vessel criticises the potter who produced it, an attitude that both Isaiah and Paul condemn as unacceptable. Paul directs his words at the one who responds with disbelief. He asks this person, "But indeed, O man, who are you to reply against God?" (Romans 9:20 WEB). However, some respond in faith; whenever they do so, their words are evidence of their faithfulness to God.

The evangelical ministry of today must express itself more confidently against oppression; it should be allowed to fulfil this God-given responsibility without being criticised for solely communicating a social gospel. This freedom should come with the understanding that it should not be criticised for doing so. Preaching the gospel and the appropriate use of the prophetic ministry are not mutually exclusive endeavours.

1:4 Because of this, the law is ineffective, and justice is never achieved; evil surrounds the upright, and as a result, justice is distorted.

The Judeans disobeyed God's commandment because He had not yet carried out His warning in the Mosaic Law to intervene to halt the flow of evil and end the oppression sweeping the land. In their courts, justice was not administered; instead, the lawless prevailed over the just, and those in authority distorted the administration of the law. These diseases were widespread across Judah.

When judges let crimes such as murder, theft, immorality, and others of a like kind go unchallenged and unpunished, God holds the whole country accountable for their actions. The sins that go unpunished poison the land, turning into a mounting debt against all occupants. Suppose God decides to ultimately foreclose on this mortgage. In that case, some inhabitants will be driven out, others will be destroyed, and new people will be allowed to occupy the land.

The response of the LORD, which comes next, makes it abundantly evident that Habakkuk was not the only one in the land offering these petitions and asking about these concerns. The prophet spoke not just for himself but also for the faithful few who remained in Judah.

The Lord's Answer

Even though God had not answered the prophet's queries in the past, He did so in the end, and Habakkuk wrote down His response. Oracles are the medium to convey this information (a divine pronouncement). The answer hoped for in response to a lament (cf. 1:1–4) would be an oracle of redemption; instead, the response given here is an oracle of judgment.

1:5 says, "See among the nations, watch and wonder wonderfully; for I am working in your days, which you don't believe even though you are told about it."

The LORD instructed Habakkuk and his people (the plural "you" in Hebrew) to shift their focus away from the events transpiring in Judah and toward those occurring in the greater context of activity in the ancient Near East. They were to see something there that would astound them and cause them to wonder what they had seen. They would see God was accomplishing something during their days that they did not believe, even if someone had only told them about it. This thing that God was doing would blow their minds.

The Apostle Paul, drawing from the LXX (the Septuagint translation) on this line, relates the concept of God's activities in Habakkuk's day to the circumstances in the church in his own day. This passage is from the book of

Habakkuk and was written in the sixth century B.C. (Acts 13:41). There is no question that God's work in using the Babylonian army to chastise Judah would have been just as remarkable as the work he did in drawing the Gentiles into his church.

"Why does God not do something about sin?" is often asked in today's society. God has taken action to fix the problem! He allowed His Son to be sacrificed more than nineteen hundred years ago. He interfered Amos the workings of the global community. He claims that He will intervene once again in the world's affairs. Yet, the world continues to have a good time while living in rebellion against God at this very moment. But God is doing something.

1:6 For, behold, I am raising up the Chaldeans, that cruel and hasty people, which marches across the breadth of the world, to seize habitation places that are not theirs.

The LORD pressed the prophet and his people to understand that He was in the process of establishing the Chaldeans as a force and strength in their world. He encouraged them to witness this with their own eyes. The word Chaldeans originates from the governing elite that resided in southern Mesopotamia and dominated the Neo-Babylonian Empire. These people were known as the Chaldeans. The Chaldean people were the ancestors of the most powerful dynasty that ruled Babylon. As a result, the terms "Chaldean" and "Babylonian." were often used interchangeably. The Chaldeans were members of the Semitic people. They descended from Kesed, Abraham's brother Nahor's son (Genesis 22:22). Even today, there are still people living in Iraq who consider themselves Chaldeans; this is particularly true of those living in southern Iraq.

Nabopolassar's ascension to the throne of Babylon in 626 B.C. marked the beginning of the Neo-Babylonian Empire's ascent to the position of preeminent power globally. This abrasive ruler inspired the Babylonians to become a harsh and impulsive country that, by the time Habakkuk lived, had already marched across the ancient Near East and taken control of other kingdoms that were located near them (cf. Ezekial 28:7; 30:11; 31:12; 32:12). God made it clear that Babylonia would serve as the rod of God's retribution for Judah, just as Assyria had been the instrument of God's judgement against Israel in the past. The prophets in the seventh century portrayed the Lord as the absolute monarch who ruled over all the countries.

1:7 They are loathed and feared by many people. Their sense of justice and their dignity are both rooted in themselves.

The Babylonians were a law unto themselves. Thus, many other countries feared and revered them. They conducted their lives according to the rules they had devised for themselves rather than the prevalent norms at the time. In the end, the people of God will be forced to fear those less deserving of their dread if they refuse to be afraid of God (cf. Deut 28:47-48; 58-68; Jer 5:15-22). The Jews living during Habakkuk's time did not believe that God would let the world's nations conquer their homeland (cf. Jeremiah 5:12; 6:14; 7:1-34; 8:11; Lamentations 4:12; Amos 6). However, their law and prophets warned them that something like this may occur (cf. Deuteronomy 28:49-50; 1 Kings 11:14, 23; Jeremiah 4; 5:14-17; 6:22-30; Amos 6:14).

1:8 Moreover, their horses are more agile than leopards and as dangerous as wolves at night. Their riders continue to charge ahead with pride. Indeed, their riders go from a great distance. They soar like an eagle in a hurry to eat their prey.

The Babylonians' military hardware represented the pinnacle of technological advancement. Their horses, which played a significant role in warfare in the ancient world, were the quickest; in fact, they were even quicker than leopards (hyperbole?), one of the species in the cat family known for their speed. When it came to attacking their foes, the Babylonians were even more eager than wolves (cf. Jeremiah 5:6). Their mounted men descended upon their foes as swiftly and stealthily as an eagle (or a vulture), swooping down from the sky to consume a prey item that was located on the ground below them (cf. Deuteronomy 28:49; Jeremiah 5:17; Lamentation 4:19). The Babylonians were compared to three different animals, all of which had similar characteristics in terms of their hunting prowess, speed, and ferocity.

1:9 Each and every one of them intends to cause violence. Their hordes are oriented towards the desert. He collects them like sand in a bucket.

The Babylonians had a strong affinity for bloodshed. As they advanced unstoppably towards victory, the expressions on their troops' faces betrayed their undying enthusiasm for conflict. They were just as successful in capturing prisoners from other nations as the sirocco (hot desert) winds from the east were pushing sand in front of them (cf. Jeremiah 18:17; Ezekial 17:10; 19:12; John 4:8). This adversary was approaching at a whirlwind's pace, and they were capturing a vast number of prisoners—almost uncountable in number.

1:10 He makes fun of monarchs, and princes are nothing but an amusement to him. Every fortress makes him chuckle because he constructs an earthen ramp and marches right through it.

The kings and rulers of the conquered regions by the Babylonians posed no danger to them in any way. They mocked them and their guarded cities, looking down their noses at both (cf. 2 Kings 25:7). They piled up dirt to create fortifications to protect themselves. They did not need any specialised equipment to take control of these towns but used the resources they discovered to construct siege ramps (cf. 2 Samuel 20:15; 2 Kings 19:32; Ezekial 4:2; 21:22; 26:8-9).

1:11 After that, he passes by as swiftly as the wind and continues. He is indeed guilty, for his might is his god.

The Babylonians were like a wind that blew across the ancient Near East, passing from one unfortunate kingdom to the next as they continued their conquests. Yet Yahweh made a guarantee that he would hold them accountable for their actions because they worshipped power instead of the one true God. To put it another way, this is why God will condemn them.

If Habakkuk had paid as much attention to the last sentence of God's response as he did to the extensive account of Judah's tormentor, he would have been able to escape the second bewilderment that overcame him, the narrative of which is recounted in the lines that follow (1:12—2:1).

When faced with a dangerous situation, it may seem as if God is oddly quiet and passive. Sometimes, He responds to our petitions in ways that are completely unexpected. And to instruct His people, He will sometimes use the most unique tools.

The concept that God remains silent despite the widespread evil in the world is the driving force for this work.

Habakkuk's Second Complaint

This passage is another expression of sorrow (cf. 1:2-4). It illustrates the issue of too severe punishment.

1:12 You, Yahweh, my God and the Holy One, dating back to the beginning of time, do not you? We will not die. Lord, you have entrusted him with the responsibility of judgment. You, Rock, have put him in the position to punish.

Power was not Habakkuk's deity; Yahweh was. The prophet's heart was filled with assurance, and his lips were filled with praise as a result of the LORD's revelation of what He was accomplishing in the prophet's day. In the form of a rhetorical inquiry, Habakkuk demonstrated his conviction that Yahweh, the God of the Holy One, existed from the beginning of time (or antiquity). The inference is that Yahweh is the only real God and that history took place as it did because the God who authored history was in control of the events (i.e., sovereign).

Since God had promised Habakkuk that he would keep the Judeans alive forever, Habakkuk had faith that the Judeans would not be utterly destroyed (cf (Genesis 17:2-8; 26:3-5; 28:13-15; Exodus 3:3-15; 14:1-6; Deuternomomy 7:6; 14:1-2; 26:16-18; 2 Samuel 7:12-29). In addition, the prophet was now aware that Yahweh had designated the Babylonians as the judges of the impious Judeans. The God of His people, who had been a rock of stability and protection for them throughout their history, had put up this adversary to teach His people a lesson—not to wipe them out completely (cf. Deuteronomy 32:4, 15, 18, 37).

Throughout the Old Testament, we find that God will often condemn one country via the actions of another nation, even though the nation being judged is guilty of wickedness. We must realise that God's ways are higher than ours and that His ideas differ. At first, this may strike us as perplexing or unfair, but we must recognise this (Isaiah 55:8-9). The execution of God's wrath is often carried out via the medium of countries. Still, God also holds nations responsible for how they behave. This is seen in Habakkuk, where God employs the Babylonians, a country with a well-deserved reputation for wickedness, to chastise Judah. Still, in the end, God holds the Babylonians responsible for their own wrongdoings. It is essential to remember that even during periods of judgement, the end purpose of God's work is always the redemption and restoration of all things. God can bring about repentance and rebirth in His people via the tribulations and difficulties that arise due to being judged. This ultimately leads His people back to Himself.

As Christians, there are moments when we may have trouble understanding why God permits some things to occur, particularly in situations in which we see injustice or suffering. On the other hand, we may take solace in the knowledge that God is in complete control at all times and that He utilises even the most trying of situations for our ultimate benefit and for the glory of Himself. In the same way that God used evil countries to pass judgment on other nations in the Old Testament, He may use the trials and tribulations that we endure in our own lives to purify us and bring us closer to Him. We can have faith that God is working all things out for our benefit, even if we are unable to understand how or why at the present moment (Romans 8:28). When we work towards following God and putting our confidence in His sovereignty, we may take comfort in the fact that God is trustworthy at all times and that He has only wonderful things in store for us.

1:13 You who have more pure eyes than those that see evil, and who cannot look on perversity, why do you accommodate those who deal treacherously, and why do you say nothing when the wicked destroy the man more righteous than he is,

Since Yahweh was the Holy One (v. 12), Habakkuk recognised that Yahweh could not show favouritism towards wickedness because He was too holy to approve of evil or to look favourably upon it. This was a fundamental belief held by the Israelites (cf. Psalms 5:4; 34:16, 21). Yet, this led the prophet to ponder an additional and more pressing question: Why did the LORD look favourably upon the treachery of the Babylonians? When the Babylonians killed people who were more virtuous than they were, why did He not rebuke them and stop them? Why did the godly remnant in Judah need to endure hardship alongside their godless Judean neighbours?

The first question posed by the prophet (verses 2-4) was prompted by what seemed to be a contradiction between the deeds of God and the nature of God.

Even though he was a righteous God, he was not punishing the sin that was being committed by his people. The seeming contradiction was the impetus for his second line of inquiry from Habakkuk. Yahweh was a righteous God, yet he let the most heinous violators prosper and even gave them the authority to punish others who had committed less significant transgressions. These inquiries demonstrated not a lack of faith but rather a confused faith. Even while it was clear that Habakkuk had a deep confidence in God, he could not understand how God was exercising His sovereignty.

Habakkuk takes his position with several others, including Job (Job 7:16-21), the singer Asaph (Psalm 73), Jeremiah (Jeremiah 11:18-19), and Malachi (Malachi 2:17), who questioned God as to His fairness. It is one thing to look at the difficulties faced by everyone who believes in a God who is both kind and almighty and to question why things are the way they are or how things can be the way they are. It is quite another thing to call into doubt the divine kindness or justice, or even the mere existence of God, for the simple reason that one does not possess the answers to these issues.

1:14 and make men like fishes of the sea, and the creatures creeping, which have no ruler over them?

Habakkuk questioned God, asking him why he had formed humankind similar to fish and other marine animals, who do not seem to be governed by anybody or be subject to any restrictions. This remark most likely constitutes the prophet's most vehement allegation against the Supreme Being. Given that he acknowledges God's sovereignty over the countries, he is forced to draw the conclusion that God is, in the end, the one who is responsible for this widespread mistreatment of people.

The larger fish consume the smaller fish, whereas the smaller fish are consumed by the larger fish. In Habakkuk's reality, the event in question also took place. Babylon was swallowing up the less powerful countries, and Yahweh did not step in to restore justice.

1:15 Using the hook, he captures them all. He collects them in his net. He rejoices and is glad. 1:16 Because of this, he offers sacrifices to his net. He burns incense to his dragnet, for both contribute to the luxury of his existence and the deliciousness of his meal.

Babylon was likened to a fisherman who, using a hook and a net, would capture other countries and then delight over the bounty of his catch. The prophet made an analogy between the Babylonians and hunters before (v. 8). On the monuments of Babylon, the Chaldeans are shown as having pierced a hook through the bottom lip of their prisoners and then strung them after the others like fish on a line. The Babylonians followed the tradition that had been started by the Assyrians.

In another piece of Babylonian relief art, the Chaldeans depicted their primary deities pulling a net into which their defeated adversaries writhed. Instead of giving thanks to Yahweh for their remarkable victories, the Babylonians even worshipped and gave credit to the equipment they utilised to achieve those victories (cf. v. 11). They have about as much respect for human life as fishermen do for the lives of the fish they catch. To Habakkuk, God acted unfairly by allowing this situation to persist.

Those who worship inanimate things by offering sacrifices or incense are not the only people guilty of idolatry. It is common for people in positions of power and affluence to show gratitude to the company or organisation that helped them achieve the desired status they now enjoy. It becomes a continual preoccupation for them, almost to the point of becoming their "god."

1:17 Will he, as a result, never stop cleaning out his net and show no compassion to the people he slaughters?

As a conclusion to his inquiry, Habakkuk posed the following question to the LORD: "Will the Babylonians persist in carrying out their sinful actions without sparing anyone?" Habakkuk was perplexed by Yahweh's policy of not dealing with Babylon's evil even more than Yahweh's policy of not meddling with Judah's immorality. Habakkuk could not comprehend why Yahweh chose to condemn the sins of His people through a country that engaged in such extreme levels of violence since this was the part he could not grasp. That is what has bewildered more [people] than Habakkuk—the acceptance and use of the wicked to accomplish the counsels of God. Habakkuk was a prophet who lived in the sixth century B.C.

That was the same issue that some of us faced when Hitler was doing such devastation in Europe, striking France and reducing it to ashes, and even seemed ready to inflict his ill will on Britain. We might accept that Britain and other peoples were being punished for their godless ways, but why should it be at the hands of the Nazis, who were the cruellest, most immoral, and most anti-Christian mob on the planet?

God can use those who are exceedingly evil to bring suffering to those who believe in him. This makes it possible for learning to take place in two different ways: first, it makes it possible to learn how to avoid engaging in one's own immoral behaviours; second, it makes it possible to realise that the activities taken by the evil agent who is causing pain are also not appropriate.

Chapter 1 Summary

The prophet Habakkuk expresses his conviction that Yahweh, the God of the Holy One, is the only real God. That history took place as it did because the God who authored history controlled the events. He also expresses his faith that the Judeans will not be utterly destroyed. Throughout the Old Testament, God will often condemn one country via the actions of another nation, even though the nation being judged is guilty of wickedness. This may seem unfair, but God's ways are higher than ours, and His ideas differ.

God's work is always the redemption and restoration of all things. He can use trials and tribulations to bring His people back to Himself. As Christians, we may have trouble understanding why God permits some things to occur. Still, we can take solace in the knowledge that God is in complete control at all times and that He utilises even the most trying of situations for our ultimate benefit and for the glory of Himself. Habakkuk questioned why the LORD looked favourably upon the betrayal of the Babylonians and why the godly remnant in Judah had to endure hardship alongside their godless Judean neighbours. We can have faith that God is working all things out for our benefit, even if we cannot understand how or why at the present moment. Habakkuk questioned God's fairness, asking him why he had formed humankind similar to fish and other marine animals.

He concluded that God was responsible for mistreating people. Babylon was swallowing up the less powerful countries, and Yahweh had not stepped in to restore justice. Babylon was likened to a fisherman who would capture other countries and then delight over the bounty of his catch. On monuments of Babylon, the Chaldeans depicted their primary deities pulling a net into which their defeated adversaries writhed. The Babylonians even worshipped and credited the equipment they utilised to achieve those victories, showing a lack of respect for human life. Those who worship inanimate things by offering sacrifices or incense are not the only people guilty of idolatry, as it is common to show gratitude to the company or organisation that helped them achieve the desired status.

Habakkuk was a prophet who questioned why Yahweh chose to condemn the sins of His people through a country that engaged in extreme levels of violence. He was perplexed by Yahweh's policy of not dealing with Babylon's evil even more than his policy of not meddling with Judah's immorality. This is the same issue that some of us faced when Hitler was causing such devastation in Europe. God can use those who are evil to bring suffering to those who believe in him, making it possible for learning to take place in two ways: first, to avoid engaging in immoral behaviours, and second, to realise that the activities taken by the evil agent are also not appropriate.

Chapter 1 Prayer

Dear God,

We come to you amid confusion and dismay, troubled by the wickedness and violence we see in our world. We cry out to you, asking why you seem to be doing nothing to stop it. How long, O Lord, must we call for help, but you do not listen? How long must we cry to you, "Violence!" but you do not save?

We know you are sovereign and in control, yet we struggle to understand why you would allow such evil to exist. We are troubled by the wicked seeming to prosper while the righteous suffer. We question how you justify using a nation like the Babylonians to bring about your judgment when they are even more wicked and violent than the people they will conquer.

We confess that we do not always understand your ways and often struggle to trust your plan. But we know you are a just God who will ultimately bring justice and righteousness.

So, we come to you in faith, trusting that you work in ways beyond our understanding. Help us have faith in you and trust in your plan, even when things seem uncertain or difficult. Give us the strength and the courage to stand firm in our faith and to continue to cry out to you, knowing that you will hear us and answer us in your perfect time.

We pray this in the name of Jesus Christ, our Lord and Savior. Amen.

Chapter 1 Questions

What is the book of Habakkuk about?

Who was Habakkuk?

What is the meaning of the Hebrew word "masse"?

What was Habakkuk's complaint to Yahweh?

What was the dilemma that Habakkuk struggled with?

What did Habakkuk turn to God with?

What is the significance of the frequency of the word "hamas" in Habakkuk?

What does the Hebrew term " conflict " mean?

What is the evangelical ministry's responsibility against oppression?

What is the message conveyed by Habakkuk's complaint?

What is an oracle in the context of Habakkuk's writing?

What was Habakkuk's hope for an answer from God?

What was the response given by God to Habakkuk?

What did God instruct Habakkuk and his people to do in response to his message?

How does the Apostle Paul relate to the concept of God's activities in Habakkuk's day?

What has God done about sin according to the content?

Who were the Chaldeans?

What was the role of the Babylonians in God's plan, according to Habakkuk?

What was the Babylonians' sense of justice and dignity rooted in?

What was Habakkuk's hope for an answer from God?

What was the response given by God to Habakkuk?

What did God instruct Habakkuk and his people to do in response to his message?

What has God done about sin?

What was the role of the Babylonians in God's plan, according to Habakkuk?

What was the Babylonians' sense of justice and dignity rooted in?

Habakkuk Chapter 2:1-20

The LORD responded comprehensively to Habakkuk's inquiry on using Babylon to pass judgment on the Jews.

2:1 I shall man my post at the watch and station myself atop the ramparts, and I will be vigilant to see what he has to say to me and what I have to say in response to my grievance.

Habakkuk drew a comparison between himself and a guard stationed on the wall of a city who was keeping an eye on the horizon in anticipation of the arrival of a horseman. A person standing while waiting for their master is in the correct posture. 1 In the Old Testament, a prophet is often personified as a watchman in several different contexts (cf. Isaiah 21:8, 11; Jeremiah 6:17; Ezekial 3:17; 33:2-3; Hosea 9:8). Under the blessing of God, the prophet and watchman could see things that were hidden from the eyes of normal humans.

Habakkuk had the intention to keep vigil and wait patiently for the LORD to respond to this second query, just as He did to the first one, so that he may tell it to his people (cf. 3:16). He got himself ready to have a conversation with the LORD about the problem. He also got ready for the LORD's response, which he anticipated would come to him in a vision or a dream (cf. Job 13:3; 23:4).

Habakkuk observes that the Chaldeans have been sent to rebuke or instruct the Judeans. Similarly, he deserves and anticipates that God will correct him regarding his uncertainties and his comprehension of the whole extent of God's intentions for the future.

The Righteous Will Live by His Faith

2:2 Yahweh spoke to me, saying, "Write the vision, and make it clear on tablets, so that he who is running may read it."

Yahweh did react, and He instructed the prophet to create a record of the vision that He would give him on tablets so that it would be enduring and simple to read (of clay, stone, or metal; cf. Exodus 31:18; 32:15-16; Deuteronomy 9:10; 27:8). The message had to be worded "such that it may be apparent to all, regardless of how busy they are or how quickly they are moving." Once Habakkuk and the other messengers had heard and documented the vision, they were to "rush" to inform their fellow residents of God's response to their question.

The text was to be written down by Habakkuk so that the reader would know how to run, which is another way of saying how to live under the will of God. This is another interpretation.

2:3 While the vision has not yet come to pass at the allotted time, it is drawing closer to its conclusion and will not be inaccurate. Wait for it, even if it may take some time, for you can be certain that it will come to pass. There will not be any delay.

The vision Habakkuk was about to have was about things that would happen in the future. Even though it was a prophecy that would not come true immediately, it would be fulfilled in the end. Habakkuk was instructed to wait for its fulfilment, as it would arrive when the LORD was assigned for it (cf. Daniel 12:4).

The words only convey the idea that the prophecy should be committed to memory by all people because of its significant role in the here and now and in the times to come.

In the same way that the order in which particular activities and occurrences occur is of critical significance in human existence, it is in the divine system of things. The seeming absence of divine intervention, which may lead to weakening faith, is, in truth, nothing more than our incapacity to recognise the time of divine action.

The author of the book of Hebrews referred to this passage in his writing (Heb. 10:37). It was a means by which he encouraged his readers to be steadfast in their devotion to Jesus Christ because what God had prophesied would finally come to pass, which in the context of the book of Hebrews would be the return of the Lord Jesus.

2:4 Look! His spirit has become inflated with pride. Even if he does not have integrity, the virtue will be sustained by his faith.

After preparing him for it, the LORD revealed His response to the prophet. This insight will be presented in the following. Habakkuk now receives instruction about the fundamental guiding principles upon which the operation of a divine rule will unfailingly progress until the arrival of that ultimate appointed time. Habakkuk's accusations are reminiscent of those that Nahum levelled against Nineveh.

The actions that Babylon took were not appropriate. Still, they were motivated by her excessive pride and her lust for evil. On the other hand, the virtuous person will conduct their life under their religion (cf. Genesis 15:6). Since she did not live by faith (confidence in God) but by sight and power, Babylon, the wicked one, would not survive to see another day. This is the implication. She tried to fulfil her aspirations by trampling over others rather than yielding to the authority God had bestowed upon him. The proud person trusts themselves, their power, their position, and achievements.

In contrast, a righteous person puts their trust in the Lord. The ungodly are those who, on a spiritual, moral, and ethical level, arrogantly disregard the way of God's righteousness to pursue the road of their own selfish wants in the day-to-day choices of life. Pride was and still is the root of all evil in the world.

The New Bible has three different iterations of this passage. In Romans 1:17, Paul cited it and emphasised the word "righteous." Both Jews and Gentiles can attain righteousness via their faith in God. Paul used it again in Galatians 3:11, but this time to emphasise the word "life." The virtuous person does not acquire a new life by keeping the Mosaic Law; rather, the righteous person obtains a new life via faith. Paul's primary audience in the Book of Galatians was Gentiles. This line was also used by the author of Hebrews (10:38), although the focus of his attention was on the concept of "faith." The virtuous are those who have confidence that God will reward them for their good deeds. The Hebrews were originally read by a mostly Jewish audience. While the concept of everlasting life is implicit in all three occurrences of the word "live," Habakkuk's verse primarily focuses on life in its physical form. As a result, this passage is a highly significant revelation in the Bible, even its primary teaching. This is the most important passage in Habakkuk because it encapsulates the contrast between the arrogant faith of the Israelites and their rescue and the prideful faith of the Babylonians and their ruin. The problem here is a lack of faith in God.

"The righteous shall live by his faith" was the slogan of the Reformation, and those seven monosyllables may very well be the seven most significant ones in the whole history of the Christian church. One definition of faith is the conviction that something is true based on the witness of others. The Christian faith may be defined as the conviction that the facts and teachings written in the Bible are true because they are based on the evidence of God.

The fundamental idea throughout the book may be summed up as follows: A faith that has developed to its full potential puts its confidence, not in arrogance, but in God's plan to create justice on earth.

Emunah, which literally translates to "faith," may also be translated as "loyal" or "steadfast." Moreover, it may refer to having integrity. 6 Did the Lord want for it to be understood that the righteous would live as a result of their confidence in God or as a result of their faithfulness to God, that is, as a result of their integrity? In other parts of the Bible, it is shown that both of these definitions, trust and integrity, are accurate. Yet, in this setting, faith or trust seems to be the predominant meaning, given that the Babylonians lacked confidence in Yahweh, in contrast to the Israelis, who did have faith in Yahweh, although to an imperfect degree. Yet, God had been dishonoured by both the Babylonians and the Israelites because of their lack of faithfulness (disloyalty or disobedience).

The difference between 'faith' and 'faithfulness' is, on the other hand, one that is more visible than real. For a man to remain loyal in righteousness, he must have confidence in God (see, for example, 1 Samuel 26:23-24); this mindset is obviously required in the current situation of waiting for deliverance (2:3; 3:16-19).

The time has come to move on from conjecture to action, from inquiry to behaviour, and from contemplating to doing one's responsibilities. As God is busy with His affairs, Habakkuk must focus on his responsibilities. It is not his responsibility to run the universe. It is a responsibility that belongs to God. Yet Habakkuk is responsible for his work, which must be carried out in a trustworthy manner. Because of this, he can live with the moral honesty and assurance that righteous living gives, even amid adverse exterior circumstances. It is the path a good man must take to survive in a wicked world.

This is the first of three beautiful guarantees God provides for His people in this chapter to encourage them. This one emphasises God's grace since faith and grace are inextricably linked. The splendour of God is highlighted in Habakkuk 2:14. We are assured that although this world is now plagued with violence and depravity (Genesis 6:5, 11-13), it will one day be filled with the glory of God. The third piece of reassurance may be found in Habakkuk 2:20, which focuses on the administration of God. God is seated on His holy throne, the King of Kings and the Lord of Lords. Empires may come and go, but God remains.

2:5 In addition, alcohol is dangerous. An arrogant man who does not remain at home and who expands his desire as Sheol is like death. He can not be pleased, but he collects from all people and gathers all people for himself.

The LORD took the idea presented in verse 4 and developed it further. When a person consumes excessive wine, it prompts them to display their pride in public. The haughty guy acts as a personification of Babylon in this scenario. Wine was a popular beverage among the Babylonians, who were famous for their love of the beverage (e.g., Daniel 5). Drinking wine causes a person to become discontent with the circumstances of his life and the things he has. As a result, he often leaves his house in search of more (cf. Proverbs 23:31-32).

The arrogant individual is never content, like death, which devours people daily and never lets up on its pursuit. In this passage, the concept of death is personified as Sheol (the grave), and Habakkuk attributes human behaviour to an inanimate thing by doing so. Similarly, Babylon gaped its mouth wide, ready to devour all individuals. The prideful individual also desires to control everyone around them, and Babylon was also notable for this trait. These were examples of Babylon's arrogance, the foundation for Yahweh's accusation against this country (cf. 1:17).

The pride of life, the lusts of the body, and the lusts of the eyes are all snares, and we learn that the one who took Israel prisoner was himself carried captive by each of them.

According to the Old Testament, Sheol is the afterlife destination of deceased people. (1) Because of this, it is sometimes compared to the grave, which is the point at which all human actions come to an end and is considered the destination towards which all human existence progresses (e.g. Genesis 42:38; Psalms 88:3). (2) To the one who lives "under the sun," the natural man, who must evaluate based on appearances, Sheol seems to be no different from the grave; it is the conclusion and complete cessation, not just the activities of life, but of life itself (Ecclesiastes 9:5, 10). Yet the Bible describes Sheol as a realm of torment (2 Samuel 22:6; Psalm 18:5; 116:3). It is a place where the wicked are cast (Psalm 9:17), and it is a place where they are fully conscious of their surroundings (Isaiah 14:9-17; Ezekial 32:21). Compare this passage with John 2:2; what Sheol was to Jonah was the guts of the large fish, and all who are within are in Sheol. The Old Testament's Sheol and the New Testament's hades are in the same place.

Woe to the Chaldeans

The LORD ridiculed the Babylonians and warned them they would be punished for their transgressions by pronouncing taunts (mocking words) against them. This song makes fun of its listeners in five stanzas with three lyrics. Then come the next five ills. Baker referred to them as the "pillar," "plotter," "promoter of violence," "debaucher," and "pagan idolator", respectively. According to the Bible, every woe is "an exclamation of grief spoken in the face of tragedy or because of imminent judgement" (cf. Isaiah 3:11).

2:6 Would not all of them take up a parable against him, and a mocking axiom against him, and say, "Woe to him who multiplies that which is not his, and who enriches himself by extortion!?" 'How long?'

Due to the crimes committed by the Babylonians, it was unavoidable that upright people would make fun of them. They would curse them for growing what was not theirs only for the sake of having more and enriching themselves by charging extravagant interest on loans. Moreover, they would condemn them for increasing what was not theirs to have more. Specifically in focus is the practice of acquiring riches via coercion and deception. 4 They questioned themselves, "How much longer would this carry on?" (cf. 1:2). When would God carry out his judgement on Babylon?

2:7 Will not your creditors suddenly spring up and stir up those who make you fear, and you will be the victim of their attack?

As they became aware of what was going on, those from whom Babylon had plundered would undoubtedly rise up and protest against what was happening. Afterwards, they would reverse the situation, and Babylon would become their plundering ground. This occurred in 539 B.C., when the Medes and Persians rose, toppled Babylon, and took control of the region.

2:8 Since you have pillaged many countries, the people who are left will loot you because of spilt blood and the violence done to the land, the city, and all those living there.

Babylon would be subject to the same retribution it had meted out to other countries in the past (cf. Proverbs 22:8; Galatians 6:7). Its survivors would pillage it since it had already pillaged the possessions of many other people. The region of Canaan, Jerusalem, and the people who lived there had been subjected to violence and pillaging by Babylon. This resulted in the loss of human life.

2:9 Woe to the man who makes an ill gain for his home so that he might put his nest on high and be saved from the hand of the evildoer!

Babylon took advantage of its illegitimate conquests to construct a secure government for itself, which it believed would protect it from any and all catastrophes (cf. Genesis 11:4; see also Obad.). 1 To become self-sufficient, it established a powerful and prosperous dynasty (also known as a "household"). There is also the possibility that the safe "nest" in question is not the residence of the ruling family but rather the nation's administrative centre.

It is not inherently sinful to save money to protect oneself against huge costs in the future (Proverbs 21:20). Still, it is sinful to save to build a fortune so that one does not have to depend on God (cf. James 5:1-6).

2:10 You have dishonoured your household by destroying many people's lives and sinning against your soul.

It was a disgrace for the Babylonians to wipe out so many different peoples (cf. vv. 5, 8). They were betraying their own best interests by acting in this manner. In other words, they were engaging in behaviour that would, in the long run, lead to their own demise.

2:11 For the stone will cry out from the wall, and the beam will answer it from the woodwork.

The stones and woodwork taken from other countries to build the fortresses and palaces of the Babylonians would be graphic witnesses to the sinful wars of aggression that brought these building materials to Babylon. These materials were brought to Babylon to build the Babylonians' fortresses and palaces. They would bear witness to the crimes of their fellow Babylonians on the day when Yahweh would bring retribution upon the city of Babylon.

2:12 Declares, "Cursed is the one who constructs a town with blood and founds a city on iniquity!"

The Babylonians should have been prepared for trouble because they had constructed their cities by taking the lives of their adversaries (cf. Mic. 3:10). The term "blood money" refers to financial gain that comes through causing the suffering of others or even the loss of their blood. The city of Babylon was constructed with "blood money" as well as the blood, sweat, and tears of individuals who were slaves. It was a town built on injustice, and without injustice, it would never have been able to develop into what it had become. While the prophet references the building of a city, he is likely making a symbolic reference to the building of an empire with his terminology.

2:13 See, is it not from Yahweh of Armies that the people work for the fire and that the nations tyre themselves for vanity?

This verse serves as the structural focal point of the whole taunt song. The fact that it centres on the LORD of armies, who serves as both Judge and Executioner, is crucial. According to his analysis, the efforts put out by the Babylonians were fruitless; he believed their labour would be for nothing in the end. Their deeds would fuel a fire that would consume them; that fire would be the fire of His judgement (cf. Jeremiah 51:58).

2:14 And the knowledge of the glory of Yahweh will cover the world just as completely as water covers the oceans.

Instead of the planet being covered in the grandeur of Babylon, it will one day be covered in the knowledge of the glory of God to the same extent as the floods cover the sea (cf. Numbers 14:21; Psalms 72:19; Isaiah 6:3; 11:9; Jeremiah 31:34). This has not happened as of yet. This prophecy relates to the eventual downfall of Babylon in the eschatological future (cf. Revelation 16:19–18:24).

In the Book of Habakkuk, the term "Babylon" refers primarily to the Neo-Babylonian Empire; since the Tower of Babel (Genesis 11:1–9), the word Babylon has had a symbolic connotation in addition to its literal one. In a symbolic sense, it stood for all of the godless peoples who, by their own efforts, ascended to greater heights so that they may exalt themselves and make it to paradise. The Neo-Babylonian Empire was destroyed by God in 539 B.C., but what Babylon symbolises will remain until God destroys it, which will happen when Jesus Christ comes to earth to set up His new order on earth during the Millennium (see Revelation 17 and 18).

2:15 "Woe to the one who offers his neighbour a drink, pouring your fiery wine until they are inebriated, so that you may stare at their naked bodies!

Since the Babylonians had fooled their neighbouring countries into taking advantage of them, God would punish Babylon for their actions. This is because the Babylonians were able to take advantage of their neighbours. The Babylonians had acted like a guy who gets a lady intoxicated with the intention of her losing control of herself and allowing him to strip her naked. The graphic clarifies that the Babylonians enjoyed drinking wine and sexually exploited their captives. Moreover, the Babylonians were known to use their victims sexually.

2:16 You are not filled with glory; you are overwhelmed with humiliation. You will also consume alcohol and put yourself in danger! You will receive the cup held in Yahweh's right hand, and shame will cover your splendour.

The LORD would pour a cup of judgment over them, intoxicating them in the same way they had done the same to their neighbours. The right hand of Yahweh is a figure (an anthropomorphism) representing His severe personal vengeance. This retribution consists of paying back in kind what the person being judged has given (cf. Isaiah 51:17-23; Jeremiah 25:15-17; Lamentation 4:21; Matthew 20:22; 26:42; 1 Corinthians 11:29). As a result of the Babylonians drinking the contents of the cup, they would disgrace themselves rather than the praise and glory that they now bestowed upon themselves.

The eventual shame of Babylon starkly contrasts the future splendour of Yahweh (v. 14). They intended to reveal their own nakedness, just as they had before exposed the nakedness of others (v. 15). The original Hebrew wording is rather explicit. It reads directly as follows: "Drink, yes you, and reveal your foreskin," which means to demonstrate that you are not circumcised. The state of being naked is fraught with both vulnerability and humiliation (cf. Genesis 9:21-25). The LORD depicted Babylon as an obscene, intoxicated man who had lost all self-control and the respect of everyone, including himself. This man was a complete disgrace.

2:17 Because of the men's blood, and for the violence done to the country, to every city, and to people who reside in them, you will be overpowered because of what has been done to Lebanon; the killing of the animals, which has caused them to be scared; and because of the devastation of the animals.

As a result of his voracious looting of Lebanon's flora and fauna, Babylon's aggression, which represented an ethical and moral injustice, would eventually come back to crush him. But, the massacre of civilians in the principal town of Lebanon and the subsequent spilling of their blood was even more heinous. Lebanon may be a metonym for all of Israel, as in other passages (compare 2 Kings 14:9 with Jeremiah 22:6, 23), and "the town" most likely refers to Jerusalem.

The One who made the world is concerned about what we now call Ecology; part of the cultural mandate He has given to humanity is to be responsible stewards of plant and animal life.

2:18 "What value does the engraved image have, that its creator has etched it? What value does the molten image have, even the false teacher, that he who fashions its shape and trusts in it producing dumb idols?"

In the same way as past prophets, Habakkuk could see through the absurdity of idolatry and expose it (cf. Isaiah 41:7; 44:9-20; 45:16, 20; 46:1-2, 6-7; Jeremiah 10:8-16). Since anybody who makes anything is always greater than what they have produced, an idol crafted by human hands cannot assist the person who fashioned it. Since the very presence of images presupposes a falsehood—namely, that they are in a position to assist people—they end up instructing us in untruth. A person who carves idols has faith in the work that he has created. Idols cannot communicate or provide assistance (cf. Romans 1:22-25).

Those living in the modern day, with all of their acquired intelligence, may believe that they are exempt from the evident stupidity of worship. What kind of intelligent and self-respecting individual would be so naive as to believe that an ancient idol's shape could be a source of supernatural abilities? But, the Scriptures of the new covenant make it quite clear that covetousness is a kind of idolatry (Ephesians 5:5). When a person's desires are directed towards the creation rather than the Creator, that person is doing the same type of stupid act as the one described above. An unquenchable yearning for things not rightfully owned is based on the assumption that objects, rather than God himself, may satisfy. Idolatry occurs when a person places more importance on the things that have been produced than on the One responsible for making those things.

Millions look up to famous individuals and consider them their "idols," particularly politicians, sportsmen, rich tycoons, and artists and actresses. Even after they have passed away, famous artists like Elvis Presley continue to have fans. Humans have also been known to worship and pay homage to man-made creations such as automobiles, mansions, boats, jewels, and works of art. Even though we can all agree that beautiful and useful things are wonderful, it is one thing to possess such things and entirely another to have such things own you. According to a quote attributed to Albert Schweitzer, "Whatever you have that you cannot give away is not truly anything you own; it possesses you." Some parents I have met hold their children and grandkids in such high esteem that they will not even allow them to explore the possibility of devoting their lives to Christian service.

Both one's social standing and one's professional accomplishments have the potential to become idols. Some individuals worship their hunger as a deity (Philippians 3:19; Romans 16:18), and their whole purpose in life is to indulge in sensual pleasures (including watching their favourite sports, perhaps?). Those who idolise their intellectual abilities and refuse to surrender to the teachings of God's Word are worshipping a horrible idol, according to 2 Corinthians 10:5.

Idolatry is founded on deceit, fosters and rewards dishonesty, and demands unwavering dedication to lying (see Is. 44:20).

Hab 2:19 Woe to the one who cries out to the tree, "Get up!" or to the stone that cannot speak, "Get up!" Will this serve as a lesson? It is covered with gold and silver, and there is no trace of a breath of air anywhere inside it.

Those who ignorantly sought to encourage their dumb idols — made of wood or stone, sometimes covered with gold or silver — to talk were cursed by the LORD, who pronounced "woe" on them (cf. 1 Kings 18:26-29). They were just lifeless works of art regardless of how they appeared or what they were constructed of. Thus, it did not matter what. It was naive to turn to any of them as a source of instruction or direction!

2:20 But Yahweh is present in the holy temple he established. All of creation should be still and quiet before him!

On the other hand, God is a living and active being, in stark contrast to the lifeless idols. Instead of dwelling in the creations of human hands, He chose to make His home in the lofty and holy sanctuary. He does not hide under gold and silver as the idols of Babylon do (v. 19), but rather, He reigns in heaven, fills heaven, and from there, He helps His people. As a result, the whole world and everything contained within it needs to remain silent and respectful before Him (fear; cf. v. 1; 3:16). There is no use in persuading Him to regain consciousness or utter a sound (cf. v. 19).

This starkly contrasts the frantic effort that man engaged in to construct "speaking" gods and the turbulent screams worshippers engaged in to make dumb idols reply [see also 1 Kings 18:26]. The inanimate deities addressed with clamour remain mute. Still, the living God approached us calmly and respectfully and communicated with us. All of the earth must remain quiet before the living God because the idolatry that causes people to forget about God and turn away from him is a problem that affects every nation on the planet. Idolatry may be summed up as paying homage to the creations of humans rather than the Creator of those creations. The things we create may be material goods, a place to live, a vocation, an aspiration, a family, or any of many other people or things. When something or someone takes centre stage in our lives and becomes the raison d'être of our existence, we are said to "worship" it. Yet, in terms of being the purpose and focal point of human life, they are just as pointless as any wooden or metal picture could be.

The Israelis did not need to be concerned about Babylon since Yahweh, who has awesome sovereignty, would take care of it on their behalf (cf. 3:16). There are times when God employs wicked individuals to carry out His greater plan for our lives. Nonetheless, He never approves of wrongdoing, and those who engage in evil are held responsible for the consequences of their acts by Him. After focusing on Babylon's transgressions, this verse shifts the focus to the good by turning to God. As a result, it serves as a transitional verse between the previous and subsequent significant parts of the prophecy.

Chapter 2 Summary

The LORD responded comprehensively to Habakkuk's inquiry on using Babylon to pass judgment on the Jews. He instructed the prophet to create a record of the vision that He would give him on tablets so that it would be enduring and simple to read. He also noted that the Chaldeans had been sent to rebuke or instruct the Judeans and that Habakkuk's vision was about things that would happen in the future. He was instructed to wait for its fulfilment, as it would arrive when the LORD was assigned for it. The author of the book of Hebrews encouraged his readers to be steadfast in their devotion to Jesus Christ, as what God had prophesied would finally come to pass.

Habakkuk also accused Babylon of taking actions that were not appropriate, but the LORD revealed His response to the prophet. The most important passage in Habakkuk is the contrast between the arrogant faith of the Israelites and their rescue and the prideful faith of the Babylonians and their ruin. This passage highlights the root of all evil in the world: a lack of faith in God. It is a significant revelation in the Bible, even its primary teaching.

The Christian faith is defined as the conviction that the facts and teachings written in the Bible are true because they are based on the evidence of God. Emmunah, which literally translates to "faith," may also be translated as "loyal" or "steadfast." In other parts of the Bible, it is shown that both of these definitions, trust and integrity, are accurate. The difference between 'faith' and 'faithfulness' is more visible than real. A man must have confidence in God to remain loyal in righteousness. Habakkuk must focus on his responsibilities and carry out his work trustworthy to live with the moral honesty and assurance that righteous living gives. Habakkuk 2:14-20 emphasises God's grace and administration of God. At the same time, 2:5-20 focuses on the dangers of alcohol consumption and the arrogance of the arrogant individual.

Sheol is the afterlife destination of deceased people, and the prideful individual desires to control everyone around them, which is the foundation for Yahweh's accusation against Babylon. The Bible describes Sheol as a place of torment where the wicked are cast and where they are fully conscious of their surroundings. The LORD ridiculed the Babylonians and warned them they would be punished for their transgressions by pronouncing taunts (mocking words) against them. This song makes fun of the Babylonians in five stanzas with three lyrics, referring to them as the "pillar," "plotter," "promoter of violence," "debaucher," and "pagan idolator". The Bible states that every woe is an exclamation of grief in the face of tragedy or imminent judgment.

Babylon was pillaged by the Medes and Persians in 539 B.C. and was subject to the same retribution it had meted out to other countries in the past. It established a powerful and prosperous dynasty and built a safe "nest" to become self-sufficient. It is not inherently sinful to save money to protect oneself against huge costs. Still, building a fortune is sinful, so one does not have to depend on God. The Babylonians destroyed many people's lives and sinned against their own souls.

The most important details in this text are that the stones and woodwork taken from other countries to build the fortresses and palaces of the Babylonians would bear witness to the crimes of their fellow Babylonians on the day Yahweh would bring retribution. The prophet also declares that the Babylonians should have been prepared for trouble because they had constructed their cities by taking the lives of their adversaries and using "blood money" as well as the blood, sweat, and tears of individuals who were slaves. Finally, the prophet believes that the knowledge of the glory of Yahweh will cover the world just as completely as water covers the oceans and that the planet will one day be covered in the glory of God to the same extent as the floods cover the sea. The Book of Habakkuk prophecy relates to the eventual downfall of Babylon in the eschatological future, symbolised by the Neo-Babylonian Empire. God would punish Babylon for their actions by pouring a cup of judgment over them, intoxicating them as they had done to their neighbours.

Yahweh's right hand represents His severe personal vengeance, which consists of paying back in kind what the person being judged has given. The LORD depicted Babylon as an obscene, intoxicated man who had lost all self-control and the respect of everyone, including himself. This led to his voracious looting of Lebanon's flora and fauna, representing ethical and moral injustice. The massacre of civilians in the principal town of Lebanon and the subsequent spilling of their blood was even more heinous. Habakkuk saw through the absurdity of idolatry and exposed it.

The One who made the world is concerned about ecology and has given humanity a cultural mandate to be responsible stewards of plant and animal life. Idolatry is a form of covetousness based on an unquenchable yearning for things not rightfully owned. It is when a person places more importance on the things that have been produced than on the One responsible for making them. Millions look up to famous individuals and consider them idols, while some worship their hunger as a deity. Those who idolise their intellectual abilities and refuse to surrender to the teachings of God's Word are worshipping a horrible idol.

God is a living and active being. He does not hide under gold and silver like the idols of Babylon but rather reigns in heaven, fills heaven, and helps His people. He requires the world to remain silent and respectful before Him, and there is no use in persuading Him to regain consciousness or utter a sound. Idolatry is a problem that affects every nation on the planet, as it pays homage to the creations of humans rather than the Creator. It can take the form of material goods, a place to live, a vocation, an aspiration, a family, or any of many other people or things. The Israelis did not need to be concerned about Babylon, as Yahweh would take care of it on their behalf. This verse shifts the focus to the good by turning to God as a transitional verse between the prophecy's previous and subsequent significant parts.

Chapter 2 Prayer

Dear God,

We come to you amid uncertainty and difficulty, seeking your wisdom and guidance. We know that you are sovereign and in control and that your justice will ultimately prevail. We thank you for your revelation to Habakkuk and the reminder that the wicked will be punished and the righteous will be blessed.

Help us have faith and trust in you, even when things seem uncertain or difficult. Please give us the strength and the courage to live by faith, knowing that you are with us and will guide us through any situation. Remind us that the wicked will ultimately be punished, the righteous will be blessed, and you are a God of justice.

We pray for the wisdom to understand your plan and the courage to follow it. We ask for your protection and guidance as we navigate the difficulties of this world.

We thank you for your grace and mercy and the hope you provide. We pray this in the name of Jesus Christ, our Lord and Savior. Amen.

Chapter 2 Questions

What was Habakkuk's comparison to himself while waiting for the LORD's response?
    What is the significance of a prophet being personified as a watchman in the Old Testament?
    What did Yahweh instruct Habakkuk to do after He spoke to him?
    Why was the message to be worded "such that it may be apparent to all,
    What did the LORD instruct Habakkuk to do regarding the vision that he was about to have?
    What is the significance of the words, "Wait for it, even if it may take some time, for you can be certain that it will come to pass. There will not be any delay?"
    What did the author of the Book of Hebrews refer to in his writing regarding Habakkuk's vision?
    What did the LORD reveal to Habakkuk after preparing him for it?
    What was Babylon's motivation for her actions, according to the text?
    According to the text, how did the virtuous person conduct their lift?
    What is the taunt song in the Bible, and who is it directed towards?
    How many stanzas are in the taunt song?
    What is the purpose of the taunt song in the Bible?
    What are the five ills referred to in the taunt song?
    What does the Bible say about every woe in the taunt song?
    What is the subject of the Babylonians' crimes in the taunt song?
    What happens to Babylon in the taunt song?
    What is the significance of the stones and woodwork mentioned in the taunt song?
    What does "blood money" mean in the taunt song?
    What is the central theme of the taunt song?
    What is the message behind Habakkuk 2:17?
    What is the main idea behind Habakkuk 2:18?
    What is the message of Habakkuk 2:19?
    What is the significance of Habakkuk 2:20?
    What broader messages can be derived from these passages?

Habakkuk Chapter 3:1-19

After receiving the vision that Yahweh would demolish Babylon, Habakkuk could see that God was acting righteously by using Babylon, a sinful country, to correct Israel. Babylon would not be set free but punished for her crimes and destroyed. On the other hand, Israel's penalty was only temporary (cf. 2 Sam. 7:16). This revelation inspired Habakkuk to compose the hymn of praise that serves as the book's conclusion. It is considered "one of the most powerful affirmations of faith and trust in the Bible."

The words of verse 2 convey the prophet's plea in its most literal form. This passage is located in the second verse of the book of Matthew. The remainder mostly comprises praise and gratitude to God, primarily for his previous acts of mercy, including the liberation from Egypt and the entry into the promised land. Yet, thankfulness is an important component of prayer, and Hannah reportedly has prayed [1 Samuel 2:1]. Still, the next song was composed entirely of a single thanksgiving.

This hymn's wording and images are similar to those found in Deuteronomy 33, Psalm 18:4-19, and Psalm 68. As may be seen by looking at the headings below, its organisation is chiastic.

Habakkuk's Prayer

3:1 A prayer is spoken by Habakkuk, the prophet, that has been put to triumphant music.

The prayer of Habakkuk is written in a hymn-like structure, similar to that of many of the psalms (see Psalms 16; 30; 45; 88; 102; 142), and according to the passage that serves as the book's title, it appears that it formerly stood separately from the rest of the book. It is possible that the prophet and subsequent Israelis performed this hymn to the music known as Shigionoth and that it was named after the tune itself. The title of Psalm 7 uses the singular form of the Hebrew word. Yet, the Hebrew word itself is the plural version of the same word. "a reeling song," also known as "a song presented in the utmost agitation" or "a song with a fast shift of mood," is a clear definition of Shiggaion, which means "a poetry with extreme sensation." If this interpretation is accurate, the Israelis will sing it zealously. In all of these examples, the term "intense" refers to an emotion characterised by a deep need for justice to be served to those who have sinned.

3:2 Yahweh, I know your great reputation. Your actions, Yahweh, fill me with wonder and respect. Refocus your efforts halfway through the years. Towards the middle of the years, make it known. When you are angry, you remember to have compassion.

The prophet admitted that he was in possession of the revelation that came from the LORD (cf. 2:1). It was primarily a revelation of Yahweh, including His justice, sovereignty, and strength; as a result, it filled him with awe. Accepting divine revelation brought forth dread of the LORD, as it should have every time.

Habakkuk made a prayer to God, imploring him to "stir up" (literally "revive") the work that God had promised to accomplish in judging Babylon, specifically to make it happen. He pleaded with God to make it clear to His people "in the middle of the years," referring to the years that passed between Judah's judgement and Babylon's judgement (cf. 2:6-20). There is no question that God accomplished this in some capacity via the Book of Habakkuk. When God was preparing Babylon for the release of His wrath, Habakkuk prayed to Him to remember Israel by showing her kindness and lessening the duration of her suffering. This occurred while God was in the process of preparing Babylon for the release of His wrath. This line is the only one in Habakkuk's prayer that asks for anything: God will protect life, provide understanding, and remember compassion. Some readers have seen it as a summary of the lesson conveyed throughout the book. It is also an expression of the underlying thought behind this psalm.

3:3 God came from Teman, and the Holy One sprang from Paran Mountain. Selah. The skies were filled with his splendour, and the earth praised him.

Throughout his prayer, Habakkuk shifted from petitioning God to praising God. He reflected on God's immense strength and kindness in delivering the Jews from Egypt, over the desert, and into the promised land. As God had previously shown his ability to save his people from the Babylonians and restore them to their country, Habakkuk had every reason to believe that He would continue to do so in the future.

In this portion of the text, Habakkuk is shown to be reflecting on God's intervention on Israel's behalf in times gone by. It is comparable to a number of the historical psalms in which the singer reflected on the history of Israel.

The prophet envisioned Yahweh rising over His people, just as the sun seemed to rise over Teman, a big town in Edom, and Mt. Paran. This peak lies just across from Teman (cf. Deuteronomy 33:2-4). While the Israelites were leaving Egypt, these places were located to the east of them. The notion here is not that the LORD will rise over these eastern areas; rather, the idea is that when He rises over His people, they will see Him in the same way that they watched the sunrise in the east from Mount Sinai when He gave them the Law. "Teman and Mount Paran are presumably designated as the two opposing bounds of the journeyings of Israel over the desert," according to a different point of view.

Elohim, which might be translated as "God," is rendered here in the single form, Eloah, probably to emphasise the inherent oneness of God, referred to as "the Holy One." Another musical notation with the meaning "to raise up," selah, may also be found (cf.vv.9,13). It most likely marks a moment in the song when the vocalists are supposed to halt for effect. This pause may have been used to modulate the key higher, to enhance the loudness, to ponder on what was just spoken, to glorify the LORD in some other manner, or to raise a musical fanfare. Alternatively, it may have been used to raise instrumental fanfare.

The glory of the Holy One spreads over the skies as the sun does just after it rises. The planet was filled to the brim with adoration due to the self-manifestation of His majesty. The Hebrew word hod, translated as splendour, most often refers to kingly power (see, for example, Numbers 27:20 and 1 Chronicles 29:25, among other places). Still, in this context, it refers to Yahweh's dominion over creation and history. This seems to be a description of the LORD appearing to the ancestors of the Hebrews on Mount Sinai. Moses used similar language to depict the arrival of Christ at that time (cf. Deuteronomy 33:2).

3:4 His brilliance is like the sunlight. Rays emanate from his hand, which is believed to be the location of his power.

The brilliance of the Holy One shone out like the sun because it was so bright. It seemed as if power was bursting out from His fingers like rays (or horns) of light were emanating from the dawning sun (cf. Exodus 34:29-30, 35). Despite this, most of His power remained hidden from view.

3:5 The pestilence and the plague went before him, and they followed in his footsteps.

When God travels over the world like the sun, He consumes everything before Him and chars everything He leaves behind. Pestilence, which literally means "burning heat," and plague, which means "devastation," are the outcomes of His smouldering holiness and evidence of its presence.

3:6 He stood, and the ground trembled under his feet. He stared, and the countries shook in fear. The once-mighty mountains have been reduced to rubble. The aeons-old hills have finally given way. His methods will never change.

God observed the whole planet as he stood there like the sun at its highest point. His gaze directed downward, like beams of sunlight, and caused the countries to shake. Just one look from him was enough to cause the everlasting mountains to crumble and the age-old hills to give way. Since His methods are unchanging throughout all eternity, He always brings about these consequences. He is a striking contrast to the lifeless idols that people worship (cf. 2:18-19).

3:7 I saw the misery that had befallen the tents of Cushan. The homes and buildings across the country of Midian shook violently.

Habakkuk saw the people of Ethiopia and Midia, who resided on both sides of Mount Sinai, shaking in dread because they saw something of Yahweh's strength. These people lived on both sides of the mountain. The Midianite and the Cushite were used to describe Moses' bride in the Bible (Exodus 2:16-22; 18:1-5; Numbers 12:1). Therefore, these two names may be interchangeable here. This may be a reference to the parting of the Red Sea by Yahweh. It should not be surprising that these individuals were shaking, considering that the mere sight of His gaze may force mountains to liquefy (v. 6).

3:8 Was Yahweh unhappy with the rivers? Was it your rage against the sea or your anger against the rivers that caused you to ride on your horses and chariots of salvation?

The prophet Habakkuk then shifted his focus from explaining the manifestation of God in Israel's previous history and the diverse responses to it to detailing the activity of God on the earth.

Using rhetorical questions, Habakkuk demonstrated that Yahweh was not upset with the rivers (Nile and Jordan) and the sea (Red) when He changed their course. According to a different point of view, the rivers might refer to all of the rivers on the planet, whereas the sea can refer to all of the oceans (cf. Nahum 1:4; Psalms 89:10; Job 38:8). As a Divine Warrior riding His Chariot, He was exhibiting His strength for the sake of the rescue of His people.

In the mythology of the Canaanites, the deity Baal confronted the personified god Yam (sea), also known as Judge River. Israel appropriated this concept but abandoned the notion that natural occurrences should be interpreted as anthropomorphic deities. Yahweh is shown as having participated in a battle with the ocean either at the time of creation or at subsequent times that are not mentioned (cf. Job 26:12-13; Psalms 29; 89:9-10).

The horses and chariots of salvation shown as the Lord riding are not the angels but the elements, namely the clouds and the winds. See Psalm 104:4.

3:9 You exposed your bow to the world. You gave the command to bring out your promised arrows. Selah. You divided the world with rivers.

Yahweh drew His mighty bow from its sheath and readied himself to shoot it. He called out many arrows to fire at his adversaries (cf. Deuteronomy 32:40-42). This is a phrase that is known for being difficult to translate. God had assembled an army of weapons and sworn an oath to them, promising to use them to wipe out his adversaries. Warriors in the ancient Near East occasionally supercharge their weapons with a mystical formula to give them an advantage in battle. The Lord acts similarly in this depiction (see Jeremiah 47:6-7). The prophet saw a vision in which rivers served as tools used by God to partition off different parts of the land.

3:10 The mountains looked out and saw you; they were terrified. The violent storm of water moved on. The ocean floor rumbled and reached its hands towards the sky.

The prophet Habakkuk gave the mountains a personality and detailed how they trembled when they beheld the LORD. He was ravaged by ferocious storms that produced floods due to the rain (cf. Genesis 7:11, 19-20). In answer to His instruction, the sea raised its waves, making them seem like hands (cf. Psalms 77:15-17, 19).

3:11 Both the sun and the moon froze in their places in the sky when they saw the light cast by your arrows as they flew and the gleaming of your sharp spear.

By His command, the sun and the moon remained still (see Joshua 10:12-13). They dimmed as He sent lightning bolts into the sky that looked like arrows and gleaming spears (cf. Deuteronomy 32:23, 42). According to a different interpretation, the arrows and spear do not relate to lightning but rather to the instruments of judgment God uses.

Hab 3:12 You went throughout the country in fury as you marched. In your wrath, you trampled the nations.

The LORD had defeated Israel's adversaries by sweeping the globe like a mighty warrior from another world. He had stomped all over adversarial countries as an animal would do when working corn. The strength of God is shown in verses 12 through 15 from the perspective of the adversary of God's people.

3:13 You went out to save your people, and you went out to save your anointed one. You brought the country of evil to its knees by crushing its head. You stripped them from head to toe. Selah.

Yahweh had shown himself to save his people in the form of a warrior and to save the one he had anointed. This might be a reference to Moses in his fights against Israel's foes, or it could be a reference to a future anointed one, such as Cyrus (see Isaiah 45:1), or Messiah (see Psalms 2:2; Daniel 9:26),3 or the Davidic rulers in general, or it could be a reference to more than one of these.

The reference to a historical occurrence (as a pattern) in the proverb "the head out of the house of the wicked" may be an allusion to one of the kings of Canaan. If this is the case, the proverb "the head out of the home of the wicked" refers to that monarch. On the other hand, if the prophet refers to the future, which is the more likely interpretation, then the king of the Chaldeans is the target of his words.

The first half of this stanza contains the information necessary to comprehend the connection between this chapter and the remainder of the book. God does not forget his promise to his people and honours it by being passive in the face of wickedness (1:2-4) or letting the persecution of his people go unpunished (1:12-17). Instead, God takes action on their behalf.

The whole point of the psalm and the theophany of God is the ongoing presence of compassionate care in conjunction with judicial intervention from on high. The prayers of Habakkuk have been answered here by God (1:12-17), who promises that his people will be delivered.

Beginning with Pharaoh, the LORD had also brought down ("smashed the head") the rulers of many wicked countries ("the house of wickedness") that were in opposition to the Israelites. He had rendered their countries incapable of functioning as if someone had slashed a person open from the bottom up or ripped a structure off its foundation. The word "foundation" derives from "foot to neck." In the same way that "head of the house" refers to the prince, "foundation" refers to the combined forces of the adversary.

"Selah." The Chaldean dynasty was destined to fall at some point in the future due to God's actions.

3:14 You wounded his men's necks with the spears they had wielded. They rushed towards me like a whirlwind to disperse me, gloating as if they were going to consume the miserable secretly.

In the act of vengeance, the LORD utilised the weapons belonging to His adversaries to take the lives of their commanders (cf. Judg. 5:26). The adversaries of Israel had surged into the Promised Land with tremendous zeal to disperse the people of God, much as those who consume oppressed people in secret.

3:15 You trampled the sea with your horses, churning the vast seas with your feet.

As though riding through it on cosmic horses, Yahweh had trampled down the Red Sea, forcing it to flood aside and create a dry route for His people to leave Egypt. This allowed them to escape from slavery in Egypt (cf. v. 8). The theme with which this part began (3:8), namely the passage across the Red Sea, returns again at the segment's conclusion.

3:16 As I heard that, my whole body began to shake. My mouth trembled in response to the voice. The putrid smell seeps into my bones, and I quiver in my position, for I am obligated to wait silently for the day of danger, for the arrival of the people who will invade us.

While Habakkuk waited for the day when Babylon would invade Judah, also known as the day that Judah would be in sorrow, he shook all over. He had no choice but to be patient as he waited for the Babylonians to become more powerful and for judgment to be passed against Israel. It is a horrible sensation to be aware that disaster is coming and that nothing can be done to avoid it.

Habakkuk would tolerate this prospect because he remembered that the omnipotent God of Israel had always defended His chosen people and promised to do so in the future. This allowed Habakkuk to find comfort in the knowledge that God would also protect His people in the future. When the prophet first learned how strong the Babylonians were, he wanted to converse with God (2:1). But now, having been reminded of Yahweh's might and faithfulness, he was speechless; there was nothing further he could add (cf. Job 42:1-6). The Babylonians would be dealt with by God. Habakkuk's only responsibilities were to wait and trust.

During my life, I have relied heavily on three passages of scripture that have taught me to wait patiently on the Lord. "Stand still" (Exodus 14:13), "Sit still" (Ruth 3:18), and "Be still" are all commands found in the Bible (Psalms 46:10). When we realise that our emotions are being "churned up" inside us, we can be confident that we need to take a step back, pray, and wait on the Lord before acting irrationally.

Habakkuk Rejoices in the Lord

3:17 Because of this, the fig tree will not thrive, nor will there be fruit on the vines; the work of the olive tree will be in vain; the fields will not produce any food; the sheep will be separated from the fold, and there will be no herd housed in the stalls: 3:18 Yet, I shall be joyful in Yahweh. I shall rejoice in the Lord, the God who has delivered me!

Habakkuk decided to thank Yahweh and delight in the God who would save him, even if things were about to worsen in Judah (cf. Psalms 18:46; 25:5; Philippians 4:4, 10-19).

The attachment of the cohortative ("I will") may be seen in both the phrases "rejoice" and "exult." This is the most forceful method to express the conviction that one will delight in the Lord regardless of what may or may not occur in one's life at any given moment. Faith is loving and serving God regardless of the situation you find yourself in.

The prophet painted a picture of the worst possible conditions by drawing on various metaphors from the plant and animal life found in rural areas. When taken as a whole, they have the effect of declaring that Habakkuk, and hopefully all of Israel, would believe in God regardless of the calamities that may befall them in the future. While the prophet had a bodily weakness, he possessed great spiritual faith despite this. Because of this, he would continue to live (cf. 2:4). When the Babylonians conquered Judah, the country, many of these terrible circumstances did characterise Judea (cf. Lamentation 2:12, 20; 4:4, 9-10; 5:17-18).

It is appropriate and fitting to express gratitude to God for his benevolence when he bestows all that is required to have a life full of health and wealth. In contrast, the ability to rejoice in God despite the absence of these other things is proof of genuine faith.

3:19 Yahweh, the Lord, is my source of strength. He transforms my feet into the feet of deer and gives me the ability to go to lofty heights. On my stringed instruments for the music director.

Even though the prophet's knees were shaking, "The Lord God" (also known as Sovereign Yahweh) was the source of Habakkuk's strength. He was the master and God of Habakkuk (v. 16). Jesus made it possible for His servant to traverse the treacherous valley in which he found himself, just as the sure-footedness of a deer's hooves makes it possible for it to negotiate cliffs (cf. Deuteronomy 32:13; 33:29; 2 Sam. 22:34; Psalms 18:32-33, 39). This bold assertion of faith starkly contrasts the prophet's uncertainties and worries, which he talked about at the opening of this book (1:2-4). His perspective shifted due to a revelation from God, and Habakkuk chose to trust what God had revealed to him.

When Habakkuk began writing this book, he was on the verge of "going under." All he could see was destruction, violence, struggle, conflict, injustice, and depravity. There was nothing else. But he called out to God, who heard his voice and delivered him from his predicament. Not only did the Lord respond to his supplication, but He also gave him the assurance that he needed to pull himself out of the muck. Habakkuk began his journey in the depths, yet he arrived at the mountain's peak. His trip could hardly be described as simple, but in retrospect, it was clearly well worth the effort.

The prophet saw that God's plan encompasses more than just his existence in a world where injustice and misery are occasionally inflicted on those who have done nothing wrong. Because of this, he was ready to give his life to the Lord and to continue putting his confidence in him.

Humbleness, devotion, and petitioning are three essential components of genuine prayer, all shown in Habakkuk's plea.

This book's concluding footnote instructs the choir director, who incorporated this chapter's reading into Israel's corporate worship services. Stringed instruments were likely chosen to accompany the singing in Habakkuk's prophecy because of their ability to create the appropriate atmosphere.

The book began with a conversation between the prophet Habakkuk and the LORD Yahweh, in which the prophet expressed his anxieties. The LORD answered with love (ch. 1). Then it moved on to a lament, in which the LORD detailed the evil of the instrument that He would use to condemn Judah, which was the Babylonians. He promised that they would be destroyed in the end (ch. 2). It concludes with a doxology, in which Habakkuk praises God and recommits himself to confidence in, and fidelity to, Yahweh—as he foresaw that difficult times were going to come in the future (ch. 3).

Habakkuk tells us to be honest about our questions and uncertainties, to take them to the Lord humbly, to wait for the Lord to instruct us via His Word, and then to worship Him regardless of how we feel or what we see. Disheartened by their current situations and/or who do not believe their lives will improve in the foreseeable future may find this book useful. It assists us in shifting from a pessimistic and even hopeless outlook into one that is optimistic and joyful as a result of the change. The most important question is whether or not we will pay attention to God and believe what He says; in other words, whether or not we will have faith.

Chapter 3 Summary

Habakkuk's prayer is one of the most powerful affirmations of faith and trust in the Bible. It is composed of praise and gratitude to God for his previous acts of mercy. It is written in a hymn-like structure, similar to those found in Deuteronomy 33, Psalm 18:4-19, and Psalm 68. It is possible that the prophet and subsequent Israelis performed this hymn to the music known as Shigionoth and that it was named after the tune itself. Habakkuk prayed to God to "stir up" the work God had promised to accomplish in judging Babylon, specifically to make it happen in the middle of the years between the Judean conquest and Babylon's expansion. He accepted the revelation of Yahweh, including His justice, sovereignty, and strength. He prayed to Him to remember Israel by showing her kindness and lessening the duration of her suffering.

He reflected on God's immense strength and kindness in delivering the Jews from Egypt, over the desert, and into the promised land, believing He would continue to do so. The prophet envisioned Yahweh rising over His people, just as the rising sun seemed to rise over Teman, a big town in Edom, and Mt. Paran, the peak just across from Teman. Elohim, translated as "God," is rendered here in the single form, Eloah, to emphasise the inherent oneness of God, referred to as "the Holy One." Selah, a musical notation with the meaning "to raise up," may also be found, marking a moment in the song when the vocalists are supposed to halt for effect. The glory of the Holy One spreads over the skies as the sun does just after it rises, filled with adoration due to the self-manifestation of His majesty. Rays emanate from his hand, which is believed to be the location of his power.

God travels over the world like the sun and causes pestilence and the plague, which are the outcomes of His smouldering holiness and evidence of its presence. His downward gaze causes the everlasting mountains to crumble and the age-old hills to give way. He is a stark contrast to the lifeless idols that people worship. Habakkuk saw the people of Ethiopia and Midia shaking in dread due to seeing something of Yahweh's strength. Habakkuk demonstrated that Yahweh was not upset with the rivers (Nile and Jordan) and the sea (Red) when He changed their course.

In the mythology of the Canaanites, the deity Baal confronted the personified god Yam (sea), also known as Judge River. Israel appropriated this concept but abandoned the notion that natural occurrences should be interpreted as anthropomorphic deities. Yahweh is shown as having participated in a battle with the ocean either at the time of creation or at subsequent times that are not mentioned (cf. Job 26:12-13; Psalms 29; 89:9-10). The horses and chariots of salvation shown as the Lord riding are not angels but the elements, namely the clouds and the winds. The prophet Habakkuk gave the mountains a personality and detailed how they trembled when they saw the Lord.

The LORD defeated Israel's adversaries by sweeping the globe like a mighty warrior from another world. The strength of God is shown in verses 12 through 15 from the perspective of the adversary of God's people. The proverb "the head out of the house of the wicked" may be an allusion to one of the kings of Canaan. If the prophet refers to the future, then the king of the Chaldeans is the target of his words. God does not forget his promise to his people and takes action on their behalf. He brings down Pharaoh, the ruler of many wicked countries. He uses weapons belonging to His adversaries to take the lives of their commanders. He also tramples down the Red Sea, allowing His people to escape from slavery in Egypt.

Habakkuk waited for the day when Babylon would invade Judah, knowing that the omnipotent God of Israel had always defended His chosen people and promised to do so in the future. He relied on three passages of scripture to teach him to wait patiently on the Lord, such as "Stand still", "Sit still", and "Be still". He rejoices in the Lord, even though the fig tree will not thrive, the olive tree will be in vain, the fields will not produce any food, and the sheep will be separated from the fold. The most important details in this text are the phrases "rejoice" and "exult", which express the conviction that one will delight in the Lord regardless of what may or may not occur in one's life at any given moment. The prophet painted a picture of the worst possible conditions. It drew on metaphors from the plant and animal life found in rural areas, declaring that he and all of Israel would believe in God regardless of the calamities that may befall them.

He also expressed gratitude to God for his benevolence and the ability to rejoice in God despite lacking health and wealth. This bold assertion of faith starkly contrasts the prophet's uncertainties and worries, which he talks about at the opening of this book. The book begins with a conversation between the prophet Habakkuk and the LORD Yahweh. The prophet expressed his anxieties, and the LORD answered with love. It then moves on to a lament and a doxology, where the prophet praises God and recommits himself to confidence in Yahweh. The book encourages us to be honest about our questions and uncertainties, to take them to the Lord humbly, to wait for the Lord to instruct us via His Word, and to worship Him regardless of how we feel or what we see.

Chapter 3 Prayer

Dear God,

We come to you in awe and wonder, praising you for your greatness and deeds of power. We acknowledge your sovereignty and ability to do great things, and we thank you for your past deeds of power in the history of your people. We thank you for your revelation to Habakkuk and for the remainder of your justice and righteousness.

We also come to you in difficult circumstances, affirming our faith and trust in you. We know you are in control and that your justice will ultimately prevail. Help us trust and rejoice in you despite the difficult circumstances we may face. Please give us the strength and the courage to put our hope in you, knowing that you are the one who saves your people and brings justice and righteousness to the world.

We praise you for your glory and power and look forward to the day when you will come to save us. We trust in you and put our hope in you.

We pray this in the name of Jesus Christ, our Lord and Savior. Amen.

Chapter 3 Questions

What is the main theme of chapter 3 of Habakkuk?

How does chapter 3 of Habakkuk acknowledge God's greatness?

How does chapter 3 of Habakkuk emphasize Habakkuk's faith and trust in God, even in difficult circumstances?

What does chapter 3 of Habakkuk say about God's power and sovereignty?

How does chapter 3 of Habakkuk express hope in God?

What is the significance of the phrase "The just shall live by his faith" in chapter 3 of Habakkuk?

How does chapter 3 of Habakkuk relate to the concept of perseverance?

What is the significance of the imagery of "the fig tree not budding and the grapes not being on the vines" in chapter 3 of Habakkuk?

How does chapter 3 of Habakkuk relate to the concept of hope?

What is the significance of the imagery of "the olive crop failing and the fields producing no food" in chapter 3 of Habakkuk?

How does chapter 3 of Habakkuk express the idea of God's justice and righteousness?

How does chapter 3 of Habakkuk relate to the concept of trust in God's sovereignty?

How does chapter 3 of Habakkuk relate to the theme of God's past deeds of power?

How does chapter 3 of Habakkuk relate to the concept of waiting on God?

How does chapter 3 of Habakkuk relate to the concept of hope for salvation?

How does chapter 3 of Habakkuk relate to the concept of rejoicing in the Lord?

How does chapter 3 of Habakkuk relate to the concept of trusting in God's plan?

How does chapter 3 of Habakkuk relate to the concept of praising God?

How does chapter 3 of Habakkuk relate to the concept of God's sovereignty and justice?

What is the significance of the imagery of the "no sheep in pen and no cattle in the stalls" in chapter 3 of Habakkuk?

Book of Habakkuk Summary

Habakkuk expresses his conviction that Yahweh, the God of the Holy One, is the only real God. That history took place as it did because the God who authored history controlled the events. Throughout the Old Testament, God will often condemn one country via the actions of another nation, even though the nation being judged is guilty of wickedness. This may seem unfair, but God's ways are higher than ours, and His ideas differ. God's work is always the redemption and restoration of all things. He can use trials and tribulations to bring His people back to Himself. Habakkuk questioned God's fairness, asking him why he had formed humankind similar to fish and other marine animals.

He also questioned why the LORD looked favourably upon the betrayal of the Babylonians and why the godly remnant in Judah had to endure hardship alongside their godless Judean neighbours. Despite our difficulty understanding why God permits some things to occur, we can take solace in the knowledge that God is in complete control at all times and that He utilises even the most trying situations for our ultimate benefit and the glory of Himself. Habakkuk was a prophet who questioned why Yahweh chose to condemn the sins of His people through a country that engaged in extreme levels of violence. He was perplexed by Yahweh's policy of not dealing with Babylon's evil even more than his policy of not meddling with Judah's immorality. The LORD responded comprehensively to Habakkuk's inquiry on using Babylon to pass judgment on the Jews, instructing him to create a record of the vision He would give him on tablets.

He also noted that the Chaldeans had been sent to rebuke or instruct the Judeans and that the Righteous would live by His Faith. The author of the book of Hebrews encouraged his readers to be steadfast in their devotion to Jesus Christ, as what God had prophesied would finally come to pass. Habakkuk's most important passage in the Bible is the contrast between the arrogant faith of the Israelites and their rescue and the prideful faith of the Babylonians and their ruin. This passage highlights the root of all evil in the world: a lack of faith in God. Faith is the conviction that something is true based on the witness of others and is defined as the conviction that the facts and teachings written in the Bible are true because they are based on the evidence of God.

The difference between 'faith' and 'faithfulness' is more visible than real. A man must have confidence in God to remain loyal in righteousness. Habakkuk 2:14-20 emphasises God's grace and administration of God, and 2:5-20 focuses on the dangers of alcohol consumption and the arrogance of the arrogant individual.

The Bible describes Sheol as a place of torment where the wicked are cast and where they are fully conscious of their surroundings. The LORD ridiculed the Babylonians in five stanzas with three lyrics, referring to them as the "pillar," "plotter," "promoter of violence," "debaucher," and "pagan idolator". The Babylonians were pillaged by the Medes and Persians in 539 B.C. They were subject to the same retribution it had brought to other countries. The Book of Habakkuk prophecy relates to the eventual downfall of Babylon in the eschatological future, symbolised by the Neo-Babylonian Empire. The prophet believes that the knowledge of the glory of Yahweh will cover the world just as completely as water covers the oceans and that the planet will one day be covered in the glory of God to the same extent as the floods cover the sea.

PART 3: Test Your Knowledge

Answer the following True or False Questions:

True or false: The Book of Habakkuk is part of the Old Testament.

True or false: Habakkuk questioned why God allowed injustice and evil to flourish.

True or false: Habakkuk was a prophet in the Northern Kingdom of Israel.

True or false: In chapter 1, Habakkuk asks God how long he must cry out for help before God will hear him.

True or false: In chapter 2, God tells Habakkuk that Babylon will be punished for its arrogance and violence.

True or false: In chapter 3, Habakkuk sings a prayer of praise and trust in God's power and mercy.

True or false: "Habakkuk" means "the one who is held and embraced."

True or false: In chapter 1, Habakkuk complains that God is slow to act against evil and injustice.

True or false: Habakkuk was a contemporary of Jeremiah and Zephaniah.

True or false: In chapter 2, God promises that the righteous will live by their faith.

True or false: The Book of Habakkuk is only one chapter long.

True or false: In chapter 3, Habakkuk recounts God's past deeds of deliverance for his people.

True or false: The Book of Habakkuk primarily concerns the Babylonian Empire.

True or false: In chapter 2, God tells Habakkuk that the Babylonians will ultimately triumph over Judah.

True or false: Habakkuk ends the book with a prayer of lament and despair.

True or false: The Book of Habakkuk is categorized as one of the Minor Prophets.

True or false: Habakkuk was a priest as well as a prophet.

True or false: The Book of Habakkuk contains some of the most beautiful poetry in the Old Testament.

True or false: In chapter 3, Habakkuk compares God's power to that of the pagan gods.

True or false: The Book of Habakkuk primarily concerns Babylonian Captivity.

Answer the following Multi choice questions:

Who is the author of the Book of Habakkuk?

A) Habakkuk
B) Jeremiah
C) Isaiah
D) Daniel

Habakkuk was a prophet of which kingdom?

A) Israel
B) Judah
C) Babylon
D) Assyria

Habakkuk wrote this book in response to a vision he received from God. What was his vision about?

A) The fall of Jerusalem
B) The destruction of Babylon
C) The rise of a powerful empire
D) The coming of the Messiah

In Chapter 1, Habakkuk complains to God about what issue?

A) The unfaithfulness of the people
B) The violence and injustice in Judah
C) The lack of rain and drought
D) The idol worship in the temple

What does God reveal to Habakkuk in response to his complaints?

A) He will punish the Babylonians for their sins
B) He will send rain to end the drought
C) He will restore the temple to its former glory
D) He will send a new king to rule over Judah

What does "Chaldeans" refer to in the Book of Habakkuk?

A) Babylonians
B) Assyrians
C) Persians
D) Egyptians

In Chapter 2, God tells Habakkuk to "write the vision and make it plain on tablets." What does this mean?

A) Habakkuk should record his vision for future generations
B) Habakkuk should create a physical representation of his vision
C) Habakkuk should share his vision with the people of Judah
D) Habakkuk should keep his vision a secret

In Chapter 2, God pronounces five "woes" against whom?

A) The Babylonians
B) The Chaldeans
C) The people of Judah
D) The Assyrians

What is the central message of the Book of Habakkuk?

A) God will punish the wicked and reward the righteous
B) God is in control, even in difficult circumstances
C) The people of Judah need to repent and turn back to God
D) God's justice is mysterious and difficult to understand

In Chapter 3, Habakkuk offers a prayer of what type?

A) Thanksgiving
B) Confession
C) Intercession

D) Lament

In Habakkuk's prayer in Chapter 3, what imagery does he use to describe God's power?

A) A lion roaring in the wilderness
B) An eagle soaring in the sky
C) A serpent slithering in the grass
D) A bear stalking its prey

According to Habakkuk, what is the source of true joy and strength?

A) Wealth and power
B) Success and fame
C) God's presence and salvation
D) Family and relationships

What did Habakkuk pray for in Chapter 3?

A. Wealth
B. Power
C. Revival
D. Healing

What did God tell Habakkuk to write down so others may read it?

A. A story of his life
B. A vision of the end times
C. The law of Moses
D. The revelation concerning Babylon

In Habakkuk's vision, what did he not see that represented the judgment of God?

A. A fiery furnace
B. A swarm of locusts
C. A flood
D. A mountain of fire

What was the reason for the destruction of Judah?

A. Idolatry
B. Lack of military strength
C. Disobedience to the Sabbath
D. Failure to tithe

According to Habakkuk, what will happen to those who put their trust in idols?

A. They will be exalted

B. They will be destroyed

C. They will be rewarded

D. They will be blessed

What does the name Habakkuk mean?

A. The Lord is my strength

B. The righteous one

C. The chosen one

D. The holy one

What was Habakkuk's response to God's answer to his complaints?

A. Repentance

B. Confusion

C. Acceptance

D. Gratitude

According to Habakkuk, what should the righteous live by?

A. Their own strength

B. Faith

C. Works

D. Tradition

Bibliography

Bruce, F. F. "Habakkuk." In The Minor Prophets: An Exegetical and Expositional Commentary, 2:831-96. 3 vols. Edited by Thomas Edward McComiskey. Grand Rapids: Baker Books, 1992, 1993, and 1998.

Carson, Donald A. How Long, O Lord? Reflections on Suffering and Evil. Grand Rapids: Baker Book House, 1990.

Darby, John Nelson. Synopsis of the Books of the Bible. Revised ed. 5 vols. New York: Loizeaux Brothers Publishers, 1942.

Dyer, Charles H., and Eugene H. Merrill. The Old Testament Explorer. Nashville: Word Publishing, 2001. Reissued as Nelson's Old Testament Survey. Nashville: Thomas Nelson Publishers, 2001.

Gaebelein, Frank E. Four Minor Prophets: Obadiah, Jonah, Habakkuk, and Haggai. Chicago: Moody Press, 1970.

Henry, Matthew. Commentary on the Whole Bible. One volume ed. Edited by Leslie F. Church. Grand Rapids: Zondervan Publishing Co., 1961.

Jamieson, Robert; A. R. Fausset; and David Brown. Commentary Practical and Explanatory on the Whole Bible. Reprint ed. Grand Rapids: Zondervan Publishing House, 1961.

McGee, J. Vernon. Thru the Bible with J. Vernon McGee. 5 vols. Pasadena, Calif.: Thru The Bible Radio; and Nashville: Thomas Nelson, Inc., 1983.

Wiersbe, Warren W. "Habakkuk." In The Bible Exposition Commentary/Prophets, pp. 411-24. Colorado Springs, Colo.: Cook Communications Ministries; and Eastbourne, England: Kingsway Communications Ltd., 2002.

Answer Guide

Chapter 1 Answers

What is the book of Habakkuk about?

The book of Habakkuk is a prophecy forecasting judgment on Judah and Babylon.

Who was Habakkuk?

Habakkuk was a genuine prophet of the LORD who could also create poetry (ch. 3). He was likely a trained prophet who worked for the temple administration.

What is the meaning of the Hebrew word "masse"?

"Masse" means "something lifted up" and describes the burden the LORD put on Habakkuk to deliver his prophecy.

What was Habakkuk's complaint to Yahweh?

Habakkuk questioned Yahweh, asking "how long" until the LORD would reply to his repeated pleas for assistance. He lamented that God had not offered proof of listening by replying to his request, even though God is omniscient and can hear all prayers.

What was the dilemma that Habakkuk struggled with?
Habakkuk struggled with the difficult dilemma of allowing evil.
What did Habakkuk turn to God with?

Habakkuk turned to God with his sincere uncertainty rather than to any other "brain trust" of ordinary humans.

What is the significance of the frequency of the word "hamas" in Habakkuk?

The Hebrew word "hamas" for "violence" appears six times in Habakkuk. This emphasises the severity of the tyranny that was taking place in Judah.

What does the Hebrew term " conflict " mean?

The Hebrew term for "conflict" refers to more than simply physical violence. It refers to a blatant transgression of the moral rule committed by someone that causes harm to their fellow man. It refers to any behaviour that violates ethical standards.

What is the evangelical ministry's responsibility against oppression?

The evangelical ministry of today must express itself more confidently against oppression and fulfil this God-given responsibility without being criticised for solely communicating a social gospel.

What is the message conveyed by Habakkuk's complaint?

Habakkuk's complaint conveys that it is important to turn to God with sincere uncertainty rather than moaning uncertainties into the ears of human beings.

What is an oracle in the context of Habakkuk's writing?

An oracle is a divine pronouncement that conveys information or a message from God.

What was Habakkuk's hope for an answer from God?

Habakkuk hoped for an oracle of redemption in response to his lament about the violence and injustice in the world.

What was the response given by God to Habakkuk?

God's response to Habakkuk was an oracle of judgment. He revealed his plan to use the Babylonians to judge Judah for their sins.

What did God instruct Habakkuk and his people to do in response to his message?

God instructed Habakkuk and his people to shift their focus away from events in Judah and toward those occurring in the greater context of activity in the ancient Near East. They were to see something there that would astound them and cause them to wonder what they had seen.

How does the Apostle Paul relate to the concept of God's activities in Habakkuk's day?

The Apostle Paul draws from the Septuagint translation of Habakkuk 1:5 to relate the concept of God's activities in Habakkuk's day to the circumstances in the church in his own day.

What has God done about sin according to the content?

According to the content, God has taken action to fix the problem of sin by allowing His Son to be sacrificed more than nineteen hundred years ago. He also claims that He will intervene again in the world's affairs.

Who were the Chaldeans?

The Chaldeans were the governing elite in southern Mesopotamia and dominated the Neo-Babylonian Empire. They were members of the Semitic people and descended from Kesed, Abraham's brother Nahor's son.

What was the role of the Babylonians in God's plan, according to Habakkuk?

The Babylonians served as the rod of God's retribution for Judah, just as Assyria had been the instrument of God's judgment against Israel in the past.

What was the Babylonians' sense of justice and dignity rooted in?

The Babylonians' sense of justice and dignity was rooted in themselves, as they conducted their lives according to the rules they devised for themselves rather than the prevalent norms at the time.

What was Habakkuk's hope for an answer from God?

Habakkuk hoped for an oracle of redemption in response to his lament about the violence and injustice in the world.

What was the response given by God to Habakkuk?

God's response to Habakkuk was an oracle of judgment. He revealed his plan to use the Babylonians to judge Judah for their sins.

What did God instruct Habakkuk and his people to do in response to his message?

God instructed Habakkuk and his people to shift their focus away from events in Judah and toward those occurring in the greater context of activity in the ancient Near East. They were to see something there that would astound them and cause them to wonder what they had seen.

What has God done about sin?

God has taken action to fix the problem of sin by allowing His Son to be sacrificed more than nineteen hundred years ago. He also claims that He will intervene again in the world's affairs.

What was the role of the Babylonians in God's plan, according to Habakkuk?

The Babylonians served as the rod of God's retribution for Judah, just as Assyria had been the instrument of God's judgment against Israel in the past.

What was the Babylonians' sense of justice and dignity rooted in?

The Babylonians' sense of justice and dignity was rooted in themselves, as they conducted their lives according to the rules they devised for themselves rather than the prevalent norms at the time.

Chapter 2 Answers

What was Habakkuk's comparison to himself while waiting for the LORD's response?

Habakkuk drew a comparison between himself and a guard stationed on the wall of a city who was keeping an eye on the horizon in anticipation of the arrival of a horseman.

What is the significance of a prophet being personified as a watchman in the Old Testament?

Under the blessing of God, the prophet and watchman could see things hidden from normal humans' eyes.

What did Yahweh instruct Habakkuk to do after He spoke to him?

Yahweh instructed the prophet to create a record of the vision He would give him on tablets so that it would be enduring and simple to read.

Why was the message to be worded "such that it may be apparent to all, regardless of how busy they are or how quickly they are moving?"

The message had to be worded so that it may be apparent to all because people would need to know how to run, which is another way of saying how to live under the will of God.

What did the LORD instruct Habakkuk to do regarding the vision that he was about to have?

Habakkuk was instructed to wait for its fulfilment, as it would arrive when the LORD was assigned for it.

What is the significance of the words, "Wait for it, even if it may take some time, for you can be certain that it will come to pass. There will not be any delay?"

The words convey the idea that the prophecy should be committed to memory by all people because of its significant role in the here and now and in the times to come.

What did the author of the Book of Hebrews refer to in his writing regarding Habakkuk's vision?

The author of the book of Hebrews referred to this passage to encourage his readers to be steadfast in their devotion to Jesus Christ because what God had prophesied would finally come to pass.

What did the LORD reveal to Habakkuk after preparing him for it?
The LORD revealed His response to the prophet.
What was Babylon's motivation for her actions, according to the text?
Babylon's actions were motivated by her excessive pride and her lust for evil.
According to the text, how did the virtuous person conduct their lift?

The virtuous person conducted their life under their religion (cf. Genesis 15:6) and put their trust in the Lord.

What is the taunt song in the Bible, and who is it directed towards?
The taunt song is a mocking song directed towards the Babylonians.
How many stanzas are in the taunt song?
There are five stanzas in the taunt song.
What is the purpose of the taunt song in the Bible?

The purpose of the taunt song is to ridicule the Babylonians and warn them of the punishment they will receive for their transgressions.

What are the five ills referred to in the taunt song?

The five ills referred to in the taunt song are the "pillar," "plotter," "promoter of violence," "debaucher," and "pagan idolator."

What does the Bible say about every woe in the taunt song?

According to the Bible, every woe is "an exclamation of grief spoken in the face of tragedy or because of imminent judgement" (cf. Isaiah 3:11).

What is the subject of the Babylonians' crimes in the taunt song?

The Babylonians' crimes in the taunt song include growing what was not theirs, enriching themselves by charging extravagant interest on loans, and acquiring riches via coercion and deception.

What happens to Babylon in the taunt song?

Babylon is warned that they will be subject to punishment for their transgressions, and their survivors will be subject to retribution by those they had previously plundered.

What is the significance of the stones and woodwork mentioned in the taunt song?

The stones and woodwork were taken from other countries to build the Babylonians' fortresses and palaces. They would witness the Babylonians' crimes on the day of Yahweh's retribution.

What does "blood money" mean in the taunt song?

"Blood money" refers to financial gain that comes through causing the suffering of others or even the loss of their blood.

What is the central theme of the taunt song?

The central theme of the taunt song is Yahweh's judgement and retribution upon the Babylonians for their crimes.

What is the message behind Habakkuk 2:17?

Habakkuk 2:17 warns that Babylon's violence towards Lebanon, its flora and fauna, and the killing of animals will eventually lead to its downfall.

What is the main idea behind Habakkuk 2:18?

The passage exposes the absurdity of idol worship. It emphasizes that an idol created by human hands cannot assist the person who made it.

What is the message of Habakkuk 2:19?

Habakkuk 2:19 warns against the foolishness of seeking help from dumb idols who are lifeless and have no power or breath of air within them.

What is the significance of Habakkuk 2:20?

Habakkuk 2:20 emphasizes that God is a living and active being, unlike the lifeless idols people worship. The verse also emphasizes the importance of being still and quiet before God.

What broader messages can be derived from these passages?

The broader message derived from these passages is that humans should focus on being responsible stewards of plant and animal life and avoid worshipping man-made creations or idols, which are lifeless and have no power. Instead, they should worship the living God and be still before Him.

Chapter 3 Answers

What is the main theme of chapter 3 of Habakkuk?

- The main theme of chapter 3 of Habakkuk is a hymn of praise to God, acknowledging his greatness and his past deeds of power, and expressing faith and trust in him, even in difficult circumstances.

How does chapter 3 of Habakkuk acknowledge God's greatness?

- Chapter 3 of Habakkuk acknowledges God's greatness by praising him for his deeds of power and his ability to do great things. It also mentions God's past deeds of power, such as the plagues in Egypt, the crossing of the Red Sea, and the conquest of Canaan.

How does chapter 3 of Habakkuk emphasize Habakkuk's faith and trust in God, even in difficult circumstances?

- Chapter 3 of Habakkuk emphasizes Habakkuk's faith and trust in God, even in difficult circumstances, by expressing his willingness to trust and rejoice in God despite the difficult circumstances he is facing and saying, " Because of this, the fig tree will not thrive, nor will there be fruit on the vines; the work of the olive tree will be in vain; the fields will not produce any food; the sheep will be separated from the fold, and there will be no herd housed in the stalls: Yet, I shall be joyful in Yahweh. I shall rejoice in the Lord, the God who has delivered me!"

What does chapter 3 of Habakkuk say about God's power and sovereignty?

- Chapter 3 of Habakkuk acknowledges God's power and sovereignty by praising him for his deeds of power and his ability to do great things. It emphasizes that God is in control and that his justice will ultimately prevail.

How does chapter 3 of Habakkuk express hope in God?

- Chapter 3 of Habakkuk expresses hope in God by acknowledging that God is the one who saves his people and brings justice and righteousness to the world and by expressing the hope that God will come to save his people.

What is the significance of the phrase "The just shall live by his faith" in chapter 3 of Habakkuk?

- The phrase "The just shall live by his faith" in chapter 3 of Habakkuk emphasizes the importance of living by faith and trusting in God, even in difficult circumstances, and the blessings of doing so.

How does chapter 3 of Habakkuk relate to the concept of perseverance?

- Chapter 3 of Habakkuk relates to perseverance by encouraging readers to trust and rejoice in God, even in difficult circumstances, and persevere through them.

What is the significance of the imagery of "the fig tree not budding and the grapes not being on the vines" in chapter 3 of Habakkuk?

- The imagery of "the fig tree not budding and the grapes not being on the vines" in chapter 3 of Habakkuk is used to signify difficult circumstances. It emphasizes that Habakkuk will trust God and find joy in him despite difficult circumstances.

How does chapter 3 of Habakkuk relate to the concept of hope?

- Chapter 3 of Habakkuk relates to hope by expressing hope that God will come to save his people and bring justice and righteousness to the world and by encouraging readers to trust in God and have faith in his plan.

What is the significance of the imagery of "the olive crop failing and the fields producing no food" in chapter 3 of Habakkuk?

- The imagery of "the olive crop failing and the fields producing no food" in chapter 3 of Habakkuk is used to signify difficult circumstances. It emphasizes that Habakkuk will trust God and find joy in him despite difficult circumstances.

How does chapter 3 of Habakkuk express the idea of God's justice and righteousness?

- Chapter 3 of Habakkuk expresses the idea of God's justice and righteousness by acknowledging that God brings justice and righteousness to the world and that he will come to save his people.

How does chapter 3 of Habakkuk relate to the concept of trust in God's sovereignty?

- Chapter 3 of Habakkuk relates to trust in God's sovereignty by emphasizing Habakkuk's trust in God's plan and sovereignty, even in difficult circumstances.

How does chapter 3 of Habakkuk relate to the theme of God's past deeds of power?

- Chapter 3 of Habakkuk relates to the theme of God's past deeds of power by mentioning some of God's past deeds, such as the plagues in Egypt, the crossing of the Red Sea, and the conquest of Canaan.

How does chapter 3 of Habakkuk relate to the concept of waiting on God?

- Chapter 3 of Habakkuk relates to the concept of waiting on God by expressing Habakkuk's willingness to wait for God and trust in him despite difficult circumstances.

How does chapter 3 of Habakkuk relate to the concept of hope for salvation?

- Chapter 3 of Habakkuk relates to hope for salvation by expressing hope that God will come to save his people and bring justice and righteousness to the world.

How does chapter 3 of Habakkuk relate to the concept of rejoicing in the Lord?

- Chapter 3 of Habakkuk relates to rejoicing in the Lord by expressing Habakkuk's willingness to trust and rejoice in God, even in difficult circumstances.

How does chapter 3 of Habakkuk relate to the concept of trusting in God's plan?

- Chapter 3 of Habakkuk relates to the concept of trusting in God's plan by emphasizing Habakkuk's trust in God's plan, even in difficult circumstances.

How does chapter 3 of Habakkuk relate to the concept of praising God?

- Chapter 3 of Habakkuk relates to praising God as a hymn of praise to God, acknowledging his greatness and past deeds of power.

How does chapter 3 of Habakkuk relate to the concept of God's sovereignty and justice?

- Chapter 3 of Habakkuk relates to God's sovereignty and justice by emphasizing that God is in control and that his justice will ultimately prevail.

What is the significance of the imagery of the "no sheep in pen and no cattle in the stalls" in chapter 3 of Habakkuk?

- The imagery of "no sheep in pen and no cattle in the stalls" in chapter 3 of Habakkuk is used to signify difficult circumstances. It emphasizes that Habakkuk will trust God and find joy in him despite difficult circumstances.

Test Your Knowledge Answers

True or False Answers

True or false: The Book of Habakkuk is part of the Old Testament. Answer: True.

True or false: Habakkuk questioned why God allowed injustice and evil to flourish. Answer: True.

True or false: Habakkuk was a prophet in the Northern Kingdom of Israel. Answer: False. Habakkuk was a prophet in the Southern Kingdom of Judah.

True or false: In chapter 1, Habakkuk asks God how long he must cry out for help before God will hear him. Answer: True.

True or false: In chapter 2, God tells Habakkuk that Babylon will be punished for its arrogance and violence. Answer: True.

True or false: In chapter 3, Habakkuk sings a prayer of praise and trust in God's power and mercy. Answer: True.

True or false: "Habakkuk" means "the one who is held and embraced." Answer: True.

True or false: In chapter 1, Habakkuk complains that God is slow to act against evil and injustice. Answer: True.

True or false: Habakkuk was a contemporary of Jeremiah and Zephaniah. Answer: True.

True or false: In chapter 2, God promises that the righteous will live by their faith. Answer: True.

True or false: The Book of Habakkuk is only one chapter long. Answer: False. The Book of Habakkuk has three chapters.

True or false: In chapter 3, Habakkuk recounts God's past deeds of deliverance for his people. Answer: True.

True or false: The Book of Habakkuk primarily concerns the Babylonian Empire. Answer: True.

True or false: In chapter 2, God tells Habakkuk that the Babylonians will ultimately triumph over Judah. Answer: True.

True or false: Habakkuk ends the book with a prayer of lament and despair. Answer: False. Habakkuk ends the book with a prayer of hope and trust in God.

True or false: The Book of Habakkuk is categorized as one of the Minor Prophets. Answer: True.

True or false: Habakkuk was a priest as well as a prophet. Answer: It is unclear from the text.

True or false: The Book of Habakkuk contains some of the most beautiful poetry in the Old Testament. Answer: True.

True or false: In chapter 3, Habakkuk compares God's power to that of the pagan gods. Answer: True.

True or false: The Book of Habakkuk primarily concerns Babylonian Captivity. Answer: False. The Book of Habakkuk was likely written before the Babylonian Captivity. However, it contains prophecies fulfilled by the Babylonians.

MultiChoice Answers

Who is the author of the Book of Habakkuk?

A) Habakkuk

B) Jeremiah

C) Isaiah

D) Daniel

Answer: A

Habakkuk was a prophet of which kingdom?

A) Israel

B) Judah

C) Babylon

D) Assyria

Answer: B

Habakkuk wrote this book in response to a vision he received from God. What was his vision about?

A) The fall of Jerusalem

B) The destruction of Babylon

C) The rise of a powerful empire

D) The coming of the Messiah

Answer: A

In Chapter 1, Habakkuk complains to God about what issue?

A) The unfaithfulness of the people

B) The violence and injustice in Judah

C) The lack of rain and drought

D) The idol worship in the temple

Answer: B

What does God reveal to Habakkuk in response to his complaints?

A) He will punish the Babylonians for their sins

B) He will send rain to end the drought

C) He will restore the temple to its former glory

D) He will send a new king to rule over Judah

Answer: A

What does "Chaldeans" refer to in the Book of Habakkuk?

A) Babylonians

B) Assyrians

C) Persians

D) Egyptians

Answer: A

In Chapter 2, God tells Habakkuk to "write the vision and make it plain on tablets." What does this mean?

A) Habakkuk should record his vision for future generations

B) Habakkuk should create a physical representation of his vision

C) Habakkuk should share his vision with the people of Judah

D) Habakkuk should keep his vision a secret

Answer: A

In Chapter 2, God pronounces five "woes" against whom?

A) The Babylonians

B) The Chaldeans

C) The people of Judah

D) The Assyrians

Answer: A

What is the central message of the Book of Habakkuk?

A) God will punish the wicked and reward the righteous

B) God is in control, even in difficult circumstances

C) The people of Judah need to repent and turn back to God

D) God's justice is mysterious and difficult to understand

Answer: B

In Chapter 3, Habakkuk offers a prayer of what type?

A) Thanksgiving

B) Confession

C) Intercession

D) Lament

Answer: D

In Habakkuk's prayer in Chapter 3, what imagery does he use to describe God's power?

A) A lion roaring in the wilderness

B) An eagle soaring in the sky

C) A serpent slithering in the grass

D) A bear stalking its prey

Answer: A

According to Habakkuk, what is the source of true joy and strength?

A) Wealth and power

B) Success and fame

C) God's presence and salvation

D) Family and relationships

Answer: C

What did Habakkuk pray for in Chapter 3?

A. Wealth

B. Power

C. Revival

D. Healing

Answer: C. Revival

What did God tell Habakkuk to write down so others may read it?

A. A story of his life

B. A vision of the end times

C. The law of Moses

D. The revelation concerning Babylon

Answer: D. The revelation concerning Babylon

In Habakkuk's vision, what did he not see that represented the judgment of God?

A. A fiery furnace

B. A swarm of locusts

C. A flood

D. A mountain of fire

Answer: A, B, C.

What was the reason for the destruction of Judah?

A. Idolatry

B. Lack of military strength

C. Disobedience to the Sabbath

D. Failure to tithe

Answer: A. Idolatry

According to Habakkuk, what will happen to those who put their trust in idols?

A. They will be exalted

B. They will be destroyed

C. They will be rewarded

D. They will be blessed

Answer: B. They will be destroyed

What does the name Habakkuk mean?

A. The Lord is my strength

B. The righteous one

C. The chosen one

D. The holy one

Answer: A. The Lord is my strength

What was Habakkuk's response to God's answer to his complaints?

A. Repentance

B. Confusion

C. Acceptance

D. Gratitude

Answer: C. Acceptance

According to Habakkuk, what should the righteous live by?

A. Their own strength
B. Faith
C. Works
D. Tradition
Answer: B. Faith

About the Author

Andrew Lamont-Turner is a theological scholar, author, and Bible teacher who has dedicated his life to pursuing theological knowledge and disseminating spiritual wisdom. With a profound understanding of the scriptures and a passion for teaching, Andrew has emerged as a leading voice in the field of theology. His extensive academic qualifications and love for God and his family have shaped him into a multifaceted individual committed to nurturing spiritual growth and intellectual exploration.

Academic Journey: Andrew's academic journey reflects his thirst for theological understanding. He holds a Bachelor of Theology, Bachelor of Theology (Honours), Master of Theology, and a Doctor of Philosophy in Theology. These qualifications represent years of rigorous study and a commitment to excellence in his field. Furthermore, Andrew's intellectual curiosity extends beyond theology, as he also possesses a Bachelor of Education (Honours) and several Postgraduate Certificates in various commercial fields. This interdisciplinary approach has enriched his perspective and broadened his ability to connect theological principles with everyday life.

Teaching and Writing: Andrew's knowledge of theology has been expressed through his teaching and writing endeavours. As an educator, he has inspired countless students through his engaging lectures and insights into the scriptures. His ability to distil complex theological concepts into accessible teachings has garnered him a reputation as an exceptional communicator.

In addition to his teaching, Andrew is a prolific author who has published several books and a comprehensive Bible study series. His books delve into various aspects of Christian theology, offering insights, practical guidance, and thought-provoking reflections. With meticulous research, clear exposition, and a genuine desire to bridge the gap between academic theology and everyday faith, Andrew's writings have touched the lives of many, nurturing their spiritual growth and deepening their understanding of God's Word.

Pastoral Leadership: Living his faith ensures Andrew takes his Pastoral Leadership very seriously. He is the Pastor of a community church in rural South Africa, where he ensures the flock entrusted to him by God is well-fed and looked after.

Read more at https://ncts.education/nctseminary/course/view.php?id=25.